PEACEWORK

PEACEWORK

Prayer · Resistance · Community

HENRI NOUWEN

ORBIS BOOKS

Maryknoll, New York 10545

ORBIS BOOKS
Maryknoll, New York 10545

Fathers and Brothers
MARYKNOLL™

Founded in 1970, Orbis Books endeavors to publish works that enlighten the mind, nourish the spirit, and challenge the conscience. The publishing arm of the Maryknoll Fathers and Brothers, Orbis seeks to explore the global dimensions of the Christian faith and mission, to invite dialogue with diverse cultures and religious traditions, and to serve the cause of reconciliation and peace. The books published reflect the views of their authors and do not represent the official position of the Maryknoll Society. To learn more about Maryknoll and Orbis Books, please visit our website at www.maryknoll.com.

Copyright © 2005 by the Henri Nouwen Legacy Trust
Paperback edition 2014

Published by Orbis Books, Maryknoll, NY 10545-0308

Portions of this book previously appeared in Henri Nouwen, *The Road to Peace,* edited by John Dear (Maryknoll, N.Y.: Orbis Books, 1998), copyright © 1998 by the Henri Nouwen Legacy Trust.

Manufactured in the United States of America

Library of Congress Cataloging-in-Publication Data

Nouwen, Henri J. M.
    Peacework : prayer, resistance, community / Henri Nouwen.
    p. cm.
    ISBN 978-1-57075-593-4; ISBN 978-1-62698-064-8 (pbk.)
    1. Peace Religious aspects — Christianity. 2. Prayer — Christianity. 3. Community — Religious aspects — Christianity. I. Nouwen, Henri J. M. Road to peace. II. Title.
    BT736.4.N68 2005
    261.8'73—dc22
                2004025699

\# 872398748

CONTENTS

FOREWORD

by John Dear

Henri Nouwen is one of the most popular spiritual writers of our time. Before his death in 1996, he published a series of small, accessible books on the spiritual life, prayer, solitude, the Eucharist, and death that have inspired millions of readers. In many ways, the focus of his writings exemplified the church's new focus on Jesus and the scriptures after Vatican II.

But what intrigues me most about Henri is that he struggled on a personal level to live these writings, to make the connection between his grand spiritual vision and daily, gritty reality, to put the Gospel into practice in his own life and so in the world. This struggle was painful for Henri, as it is for everyone. It meant taking risks, moving on, and seeking God's place for him in the world. A Dutch priest and psychologist, he became a popular author and speaker, as well as a favorite professor at Notre Dame, Yale, and Harvard. But then, at the height of his career, he walked away from the academic world. After exploring the possibility of life among the Trappists or as a missionary in Latin America, he moved to Toronto and joined the L'Arche Daybreak community to serve people with disabilities. Henri tried to engage the world by living and applying Gospel values. For me, that rare application makes all the difference toward a more authentic spirituality and spiritual life.

Henri Nouwen faced the world of pain and violence without blinking. He looked it in the eye and offered it a word of love, healing, and peace, which at first glance might appear to be sentimental, but was actually rooted in a firm social, political spirituality. He knew that as a follower of Jesus he had to seek first God's reign of peace and justice, and that his spiritual writings had to reflect all the aspects of God's reign — not just personal salvation, but also social and global transformation. It is this wide viewpoint that makes Henri's writing unique.

There are many books on spirituality, many spiritual teachers, and many ways to pursue the so-called "spiritual life." But as a Jesuit trying to work for peace and justice over the last twenty-five years, I find that most miss the mark because they do not address the global crises of war, nuclear weapons, poverty, hunger, AIDS, and the threat of environmental destruction. These so-called "political issues" are matters of life and death, which means they are first and foremost spiritual matters. That is why Jesus dedicated himself so passionately to justice for the poor and a vision of God's reign of peace on earth, and why he gave his life to the formation of a community of peacemakers who would confront institutionalized, imperial injustice head on, just as he did.

Publicly resisting evil and making peace in the world are at the heart of every authentic spirituality. Unfortunately, few of us make this critical connection between the spiritual life on the one hand, and war, poverty, and nuclear weapons on the other. Most of us disconnect our private spiritual experience from "the real world" of business, electoral politics, bombing raids, and national "security." Perhaps we do not want to cause trouble, divide our congregations, or risk the charge of being unpatriotic. Yet, without realizing it, our passivity and silence in the face of global violence renounces the prophetic witness of the nonviolent Jesus. Rather than align ourselves with God's reign of justice and peace, we opt for the status quo of war and global injustice. It is as if, in order to write or speak about prayer and spirituality today, we have to ignore the war in Iraq, or the violence in the Middle East, or the ongoing development of nuclear weapons at Los Alamos, while in the meantime budgets for schools, jobs, homes, food, and health care are slashed. The culture tells us that these issues, painful as they may be, do not concern our spiritual life, that there is no connection between our private prayer and the horrors we read about in the morning paper.

With this book, Henri insists that there is a connection. He links his personal experience of God, his insights into pastoral psychology, and his understanding of Christian discipleship, not only with the poor and the broken around us, but with the global injustices of our times. For Henri these insights were the fruit of a personal journey that began long before he wrote this book and that continued until the day he died.

In the 1960s, Henri drove south to join Dr. King and many others in the heroic march in Selma that marked a turning point in the civil rights struggle; later he returned to walk with the thousands at Dr. King's funeral. In the 1970s, he spoke at antiwar rallies and kept vigil for peace at a Trident submarine base in Connecticut. In the 1980s he journeyed to the war zones of Nicaragua and Guatemala, toured the country to speak out against Reagan's contra war and the nuclear arms race, and joined protesters at the Nevada Nuclear Weapons Test Site. On January 14, 1991, on the eve of the first Gulf War, Henri addressed ten thousand people in Washington, D.C., denouncing the impending war and calling Christians to take a stand for peace. "I have become more aware than ever," he wrote me shortly afterward, "of how hard it is to proclaim radically the peace of Jesus in a world that so quickly gravitates to violent solutions of its problems."

Henri knew that the spiritual life summoned him to work for peace, that if he was to fulfill his vocation to be a beloved son of God, he had to be a peacemaker, a voice for peace in a world of war. In the early 1990s, when I was in prison for an antinuclear demonstration, Henri wrote long supportive letters telling me that he too was trying to stand for peace, that he consciously saw his work at L'Arche as a witness against war and nuclear weapons, and that he wanted to be part of the growing movement for nonviolence and disarmament. He even wrote to me about the possibility of risking arrest and imprisonment himself in order to make clear his nonviolent resistance to wars and weaponry. I think Henri's willingness to stand for peace and justice is still widely misunderstood, if not deliberately ignored. For me, however, this stand makes a crucial difference. That's what gives his writing integrity — his personal grounding among the poor and the marginalized, his real solidarity with the movements for justice and peace, and his public stand against the many wars of his time.

Henri Nouwen tried to live a life of peace, to promote the vision of peace, and to teach the way of peace. In the early 1980s, in the midst of escalating Cold War tensions, he wrote this short book as his contribution to the church and the peace movement, so that those marching and advocating peace would root their actions in the heart of peace: in Jesus, who is the face of the God of peace, and in his Holy Spirit. He did not address the political landscape as much as the inner spiritual landscape. He thought that the only way to help pull humanity back from the brink of global destruction was through an inner conversion of heart followed by social, political, and economic transformation.

Though parts of this manuscript were published in a small church journal, Henri never got around to publishing the full text. In *The Road to Peace*, published after Henri's sudden death in 1996, I gathered his available writings on peace and justice, including much of this manuscript. But the complete text of *Peacework*, including the chapter on community and the final conclusion, are published now for the first time.

Had Henri lived, he might well have updated or revised this text or added other ingredients to his spirituality of peacemaking. A few years after moving to L'Arche, he wrote a little booklet titled "The Path of Peace," where he continued to grapple with the spirituality of peace. There, along with prayer, resistance, and community, he added a further ingredient: receiving the gift of peace from the weak, the broken, the poor, and the marginalized. It was a lesson drawn from his experience at L'Arche and particularly from his relationship with Adam, a severely disabled young man in the Daybreak community. The poor teach us about the sufferings and injustices of the world, Henri explained, but most of all, they share with us God's gift of peace, a gift of which they are the first recipients, according to the Beatitudes. (That booklet, included in the collection *Finding My Way Home,* could well be read along with the present volume to round out Henri's spirituality of peacemaking.)

In these difficult times of fear, anxiety, war, and terrorism, Henri's message of peace is needed more than ever. Though written twenty years ago, his description of "the house of fear" remains an apt definition for the world today. In words that have taken on a new urgency he calls us to leave the house of fear and to journey toward the house of love and peace. And he invites us all to work for peace through prayer, resistance, and community.

Although his spirituality of peace might be dismissed in the post–September 11 world as impractical, naïve, and idealistic, Henri writes from a biblical perspective. As a spiritual seeker and guide, Henri knew that God is a God of peace and therefore that God wants us to "beat our swords into plowshares" and "study war no more." He saw that Jesus walked the path of peace and wanted his disciples to become peacemakers like him. As he announced in the Sermon on the Mount, "Blessed are the peacemakers, for they will be called children of God." These words "have become the key words for our lives as Christians today," Henri writes boldly in his conclusion. If we want to grow into a mature spirituality and become authentic disciples of Jesus, we have to take a stand against the culture of war and become peacemakers, he explains, regardless of what others may say. "To live a life in the Spirit of Christ today," Henri concludes, means "to opt for a way of being in the world that in no way pays tribute to the forces of destruction." Nothing in the years since Henri wrote these words has dimmed the urgency of that challenge.

I hope many readers will ponder Henri's meditations, take them to heart, and reclaim the wisdom of peace with all its social and political implications. Most importantly, I hope these readers will undertake bold new steps for peace — as Henri did, by publicly speaking out against war, demonstrating against nuclear weapons, and joining the movements for nonviolent social change. As Henri's life shows, if we dare to embark on this spiritual journey and enter the fray as a presence and a voice for peace, our spirituality will only deepen and our lives will bear good fruit.

If we practice the Gospel spirituality of peace and non-violence, as Henri teaches, we will discover that we are indeed God's beloved sons and daughters. That blessing of Christ's peace is what the spiritual life is all about.

JOHN DEAR

Feast of St. Francis of Assisi
October 4, 2004
Madrid, New Mexico

INTRODUCTION

Long enough have I been dwelling
with those who hate peace.
I am for peace, but when I speak,
they are for fighting.

(Psalm 120:6–7)

On August 6, 1945, the day on which the atom bomb was first used in war, peacemaking came to mean what it could not have meant before: the task of saving humanity from collective suicide. On August 6, 1945, while Christians celebrated the Transfiguration of Jesus on Mount Tabor, the nuclear era was inaugurated by a light that incinerated Hiroshima and killed 125,000 of its inhabitants. On that day the blessing on peacemakers became the blessing for our century. The bombing of Hiroshima and the nuclear arms race that followed have made peacemaking the central task for Christians. There are many other urgent tasks to accomplish: the work of worship, evangelization, healing of church divisions, alleviating worldwide poverty and hunger, and defending human rights. But all of these tasks are closely connected with the task that stands above

them all: making peace. Making peace today means giving a future to humanity, making it possible to continue
our life together on this planet.

Every one of the eight beatitudes that Jesus proclaimed
in the Sermon on the Mount is for all people and for
all times. But there are times in which one word speaks
louder than another. In the thirteenth century St. Francis
brought to the foreground the blessing on the poor. In
the nineteenth century many saints and visionaries called
new attention to the blessing on the pure of heart. Clearly
our century is the century of the peacemakers. Qoheleth
says: "There is a season for everything, a time . . . a time
for keeping silent, a time for speaking . . . a time for war,
a time for peace" (Eccles. 3:1, 7–8). This is the time to
speak for peace. If we do not recognize this, there will be
no seasons anymore for anything, because without peace
there will be no life. If this century will be remembered,
it will be remembered for those who gave themselves for
the cause of peace.

In these reflections I hope to show how peacemaking
can no longer be regarded as peripheral to being a Christian. It is not something like joining the parish choir.
Nobody can be a Christian without being a peacemaker.
The issue is not that we have the occasional obligation
to give some of our attention to war prevention, or even
that we should be willing to give some of our free time to
activities in the service of peace. What we are called to is a
life of peacemaking in which all that we do, say, think, or
dream is part of our concern to bring peace to this world.
Just as Jesus' command to love one another cannot be seen

as a part-time obligation, but requires our total invest-ment and dedication, so too Jesus' call to peacemaking is unconditional, unlimited, and uncompromising. None of us is excused! It isn't something limited to specialists who are competent in political and military matters, or to the radicals who have dedicated themselves to leaflet-ing, demonstrating, and civil disobedience. No specialist or radical can diminish the undeniable vocation of each Christian to be a peacemaker. Peacemaking is a full-time vocation that includes each member of God's people.

How would the world look if all Christians — in Aus-tralia, Asia, Europe, Africa, North and South America — were to commit themselves without reservation to peace? How would the world look if all Christians — young, middle-aged, or old — were to say loudly and clearly in words and deed: "We are for peace"? And how would the world look if all Christians — Protestant, Catholic, Orthodox — were to witness together for him who is the Prince of Peace, Jesus? What would such a consensus in conscience bring about? Would we still spend billions of dollars every month to build ingenious instruments of death while millions of people are starving? Would we still live with the constant fear of impending holocaust? Would we still hear about parents who doubt if it is responsible to bring children into this world and about children who wonder if they will live to grow old?

The tragedy is that, in some demonic way, the word "peace" has become tainted. For many people this most precious word has become associated with sentimental-ism, utopianism, radicalism, romanticism, and even with irresponsibility. The remark "You are for peace" often seems to mean "You are a dreamer." When a plea is made to invest time, money, and energy in creating a Department for Peace many smile and dismiss the idea as belonging to people who really do not have both feet on the ground. And when the opportunity presents itself to build a port for the Trident submarine, many are more concerned with creating new jobs than with preventing a new war.

"If I speak of peace, they are for fighting." These words are more real than ever. Every day newspapers, radio, and television broadcasts reveal our unashamed desire to show our teeth, to fight, and to be the strongest superpower. Genuine words of peace are not often heard in our world and when spoken they are mostly distrusted. When said by the enemy they are dismissed as "mere propaganda." While the word "freedom" has become a word uttered with self-confidence, the word "peace" is said timidly and often with the fear of being considered disloyal and untrustworthy.

Must it remain this way? Must war drums constantly disturb us? Must we hear over and over that we need more and stronger weapons to safeguard our values and our lives? Must we listen to unsettling speeches saying that ten thousand strategic and twenty-two thousand tactical nuclear weapons, enough to destroy every major Russian city forty times over, are not enough? Must we let our minds be occupied with the destructive possibilities of intercontinental ballistic missiles, B-52 bombers, and Trident submarines? And must we even discuss the acceptability of the death of 15 million people in a limited nuclear war? Must we go on preparing for the greatest mass murder in history?

We have been dwelling with those who hate peace long enough. Long enough have we allowed ourselves to be impressed by "the rulers, the governors and the commanders, the rich people and the men of influence" (Rev. 6:15) who try to tell us that the political situation is too complex for us to have an opinion about the possibility and desirability of peace, and who try to convince us that the science of defense is too advanced for us really to understand. Long enough have we been kept silent about those who are for war and are eager to see the demonic products of their intelligence put to use. But when we cry out: "We are for peace, we are for peace," our words sound so incompetent, simplistic, and naïve. The sophisticated arguments of those who say the issues of war and peace are too complex for us to understand seduce us into feelings of powerlessness and uselessness.

The truth, however, may be simple after all. Maybe the difficult grammar of warmaking, with words such as fusion and fission, MAD, MARV, and MX, is nothing more than an elaborate screen hiding the face of the One who says: "You must love the Lord your God with all your heart, with all your soul, with all your strength, and with all your mind and your neighbors as yourself" (Luke 10:27). It is a simple but hard truth, requiring constant vigilance, resolution, and practice. This difficult truth, the truth of peace, has to be spoken and lived —

directly, courageously, intelligently, gently, lovingly, and repeatedly.

It is far from easy to write on this subject. For a long time I have sensed within me a strong hesitation to speak or write about peace. I have been dwelling for so long in the houses of those who look at protest and peace movements as expressions of youthful rebellion or anti-patriotism that I feel embarrassed to say openly, "I am for peace." Much of this hesitation goes back to my time spent in the Dutch army. Although the seminary had kept me out of military service, I felt that a seminarian should not be exempt from the experience other Dutch men share: two years of uniformed service for their country. So I volunteered to become an army chaplain, took some basic training, and worked as a priest-psychologist on a military mental health team. I have very fond memories of those days. I enjoyed the "team spirit," came to know people I never would have met otherwise, learned a lot about psychology, felt very useful, and made closer friends than during my six years in the seminary.

To be a conscientious objector seemed understandable for certain small sects, but unnatural for "normal" Catholics and Protestants. It was good to defend your country, and no "real man" would try to escape from that duty. Moreover, I liked the uniform: it looked a lot more impressive than my black suit with Roman collar! But later, during the Vietnam years, I found myself in the United States. A personal friendship with an officer who refused further service and risked going to prison slowly changed my attitude. Those who objected to the U.S. involvement in Vietnam no longer seemed selfish cowards or sentimental dreamers but people who had found the war immoral, illegal, and unjust and dared to act according to their convictions. While counseling war resisters, I received a letter from the chaplaincy office of the Dutch army, announcing that it had pleased Queen Juliana to promote me to major in Her Majesty's Army (on reserve!). When I read that letter I felt a confusing mixture of embarrassment and pride.

However, it wasn't only my Dutch army experience that made me hesitant to join the peace movement. My observations of the style, language, and behavior often exhibited at antiwar rallies in the 1960s had made me skeptical about the value of much antiwar activity. The many conflicts and divisions among peacemakers evoked an inner distaste in me and renewed my respect for the cleanliness, orderliness, discipline, and single-mindedness of those who served their country in the military. Even today, having become deeply convinced of the immorality of the fabrication, possession, and use of nuclear weapons, I still feel quite nervous about speaking or acting for peace, especially when it brings me into the company of those whose personal style, ideology, and tactics are totally alien to me.

But all these memories and emotions do not diminish the truth that the call to peace is a call for all people regardless of the many differences, regardless of their ideologies, ethnic backgrounds, religious connections, and social conditions — regardless even of "taste and manners." Jesus said: "Blessed are the peacemakers, for they will be called children of God" (Matt. 5:9). These words can no longer remain in the background of our Christian consciousness. These words are breaking into our lives with such urgency that we know that this is the time, even the hour, to say together, "We are for peace."

Christians today, if they want to be Christians, have to find the courage to make the word "peace" as important as the word "freedom." There should be no doubt in the minds of the people who inhabit this world that Christians are peacemakers.

I say this so simply and directly precisely because I am so aware of the many questions that have often kept Christians divided. Some adopt the just-war theory; others argue for pacifism. Many books and articles have been written on such important issues as non-violence, conscientious objection, and civil disobedience; I am hopeful that there will be less disagreement among Christians as the discussion develops. But it would be a tragedy if the divergence of opinion on these issues were to prevent the people of God from witnessing clearly and convincingly for peace. The urgency of the need for peacemaking today must allow us to speak and act in spiritual unity, even when many concrete issues of tactics and strategy remain open for further discussion. I therefore am not focusing here on what remains to be worked out, but rather on what gives us the power to speak and act together *now* in preventing a global holocaust.

Thus I say: Peacemaking belongs to the heart of our Christian vocation; peacemaking is a full-time task for all Christians; and peacemaking has become in our century the most urgent of all Christian tasks. These statements explain why I want to help develop a spirituality of peacemaking.

From the perspective of the Christian tradition I won't say anything that has not been said before. From the perspective of the urgency of the need for peacemaking I will say things that are quite new. Therefore these reflections ask little and much at the same time. I am not asking for involvement in any specific organization or project. I am not even suggesting any specific change in our work or family life. But I am asking for a conversion of our whole person so that all we do, say, and think becomes part of our urgent vocation to be peacemakers. Such a conversion can indeed lead to change and specific actions, but it can also make us live the same life in a totally new way.

For whom do I write? For all who want to be peacemakers: whether you live on a farm or in a skyscraper, whether you work in a factory or in a university, whether you are hidden in a contemplative monastery or visible in the street. Peacemaking is not restricted by any schedule, job, or talent. It is as universal a calling as the call to love. I am writing primarily for Christians, but hope that others can also recognize the vocation to be a peacemaker as a vocation for all people. Most of all I am writing for particular friends, men and women I have come to know and to love deeply during the past decades. Some have radically committed themselves to peacemaking with great sacrifices for their families, careers, and freedom of movement. A few have dedicated themselves fully to contemplative peacework. Many are still struggling to find their own vocation in the service of peace. All of them are part of this little book. I trust that their presence in my life will make these reflections concrete and specific enough to touch not only those who are in the thick of the struggle but also those who still stand hesitantly at a distance.

I have developed these reflections on peacemaking around three themes: prayer, resistance, and community. It is nothing new to say that we all have to pray to resist evil and to live together in love. There is hardly any spiritual book that does not say this in one way or another, and I want to say it again. But I want to say this against the background of a world poised for self-destruction, a world in which the choice no longer is between peace and war, but between peace and the end of history. In such a world, the age-old call to prayer, resistance, and community truly becomes a new call.

I

PRAYER

There is one thing I ask of the Lord;
for this I long;
To live in the house of the Lord
all the days of my life,...

For there God keeps me safe in God's tent.
In the day of evil God hides me.
In the shelter of God's tent on a rock
God sets me safe....

And now my head shall be raised
above my foes who surround me.
And I shall offer within God's tent
a sacrifice of joy.

(Psalm 27:4, 5, 6)

Where Are We Staying?

A peacemaker prays. Prayer is the beginning and the end, the source and the fruit, the core and the content, the basis and the goal of all peacemaking. I say this without apology, because it allows me to go straight to the heart of the matter, which is that peace is a divine gift, a gift we receive in prayer.

In his farewell discourse Jesus said to his apostles, "Peace I leave to you, my own peace I give to you; a peace the world cannot give, this is my gift to you" (John 14:27). When we want to make peace we first of all have to move away from the dwelling places of those who hate peace and enter into the house of him who offers us his peace. This entering into a new dwelling place is what prayer is all about. The question indeed is: "Where are you staying? To whom do you belong? Where is your home?" Praying is living in the House of the Lord. There "he keeps me safe...in the day of evil" and there "my head shall be raised above my foes" (Ps. 27). First we need to prevent ourselves from being seduced by those who prepare for the day of destruction and the end of all things. "Watch yourselves," Jesus said,

> or your hearts will be coarsened with debauchery and drunkenness and the cares of life and that day will be sprung on you suddenly like a trap. For it will come down on every living person on the face of the earth. Stay awake, praying at all times for the strength to survive all that is going to happen and to stand with confidence before the Son of Man.
>
> (Luke 21:34–36)

"Praying at all times" is the first aspect of peacemaking. What does this mean concretely for us who have barely enough time and space to keep some distance from the cares of life? To answer this question we must first be willing to explore critically the ways in which the "cares of life" strangle us. Only then can we see the converting power of prayer and its pervasive role in peacemaking.

Wounds and Needs

As I reflect on our daily human behavior I am over-whelmed by how needy we are. Wherever we look we see our needs at work: the need for attention, for affection, for influence, for power, and most of all the need to be considered worthwhile. When we explore honestly why we do what we do, say what we say, and think what we think we discover — to our own horror — that even our most generous actions, words, and fantasies are entangled with these needs.

When we go to comfort a friend we find ourselves wondering if he will appreciate our visit. When we spend time and money to fight hunger and oppression in the world, we find ourselves subtly concerned about recognition and praise. When we listen with great attentiveness to the stories of those who come for help, we find ourselves often caught in the trap of sensationalism and curiosity. And even when we speak with fervor and conviction about the humility and patience of Jesus, we cannot avoid a strong desire to put ourselves at the center of attention. Thus we have to confess that much of our behavior — even our so-called good behavior — is an anxious, though perhaps unconscious, attempt to advance our own cause, to make ourselves known and to convince our world that we need to be reckoned with. This is the "goodness" of sinners that Jesus so fiercely criticizes.

If you love those who love you, what thanks can
you expect? Even sinners love those who love them.
And if you do good to those who do good to you,
what thanks can you expect? For even sinners do
that much. And if you lend to those from whom you
hope to receive, what thanks can you expect? Even
sinners lend to sinners to get back the same amount.
(Luke 6:32–34)

Why is it so hard to go beyond this strange moral exchange in which every good deed has a price attached
to it? Why is it that our needs often spoil even the most
altruistic gestures? Our needs for affection, attention, influence, and power are anchored in very old and often
deeply hidden wounds. These wounds can be inflicted by
experiences of being disliked, unappreciated, or even rejected. They can be attached to concrete events in the past,
to vague memories, or to overheard stories. They can be
connected with our families, teachers, or friends. They
can be very specific or very global. But somehow, somewhere they make us wonder if we are really worth being.
It is this fundamental inner doubt about our own value
that catapults us into a search for self-esteem so loaded
with apprehension that it easily becomes compulsively
egocentric and even destructive.

When I listen to the sounds of greed, violence, rape,
torture, murder, and indiscriminate destruction, I hear a
long, sustained cry coming from all the corners of the
world. It is the cry of a deeply wounded humanity that no

longer knows a safe dwelling place but wanders around the planet in a desperate search for love and comfort.

Needs that are anchored in wounds cannot be explained simply. Even though we often point an accusing finger at someone whom we consider the cause of our problem and even though we often make ourselves believe that things could have been different if only that someone had done or said something differently, we are part of a chain of wounds and needs that reach far beyond our memories and aspirations. Our unquenchable need to be loved may be connected with an experience of rejection in our early months of life. Still, weren't our parents subject to wounds and needs too, wounds and needs that go back to their parents and grandparents and through them far into the most hidden recesses of the past? And we, in turn, may have a strong desire to be blameless in the eyes of our children and friends, to not hurt them, and to keep the pain that we have suffered far from them. Yet we will come to the painful realization that they too will feel wounded and carry on in their lives a search for a love we could not provide, a search stretching out into the far reaches of the future. This is the pervasive tragedy of humanity, the tragedy of an experience of homelessness that winds through history and is passed by each generation to the next in a seemingly unending sequence of human conflicts with even more destructive tools of rage in our hands. The vicious repetition of wounds and needs creates the milieu of "those who hate peace." It is the dwelling place of demons. And it is a place that lures us precisely because we all are wounded and needy.

It can indeed come as a great shock to realize that what we consider works of service in the name of God may be motivated to such a degree by our wounds and needs that not peace, but resentment, anger, and even violence become their fruits. The great irony is that Satan finds his safest hiding place where we are most explicitly involved in the work of God's kingdom. The "enemy... prowling round like a roaring lion, looking for someone to eat" (1 Pet. 5:8–9) is often very successful when and where we least expect him. We must consider this seriously. If we cannot see the dark works of conflict and war in our own daily lives, we will never fully understand the cruelty, torture, and mass murder that fill the pages of our newspapers day after day. The name of God is used for many demonic actions. It is the safest mask of Satan and we have to continually tear it off if we want to be peacemakers. Though it might be easy to recognize the forces of darkness around us, it is very hard to recognize these same forces in our own "good works." Self-doubt, inner restlessness, fear of being left alone, need for recognition, and desire for fame and popularity are often stronger motives in our actions for peace than true passion for service. These are the motives that bring elements of war into the midst of our action for peace.

Only when we are willing repeatedly to confess that we too have dirty hands, even when we work for peace, can we fully understand the hard task of peacemaking.

The great spiritual tragedy is that many cruel and inhuman acts are committed in the name of serving God. After the atom bomb was successfully exploded above

Hiroshima, President Truman wrote: "We thank God that it [the bomb] has come to us . . . and we pray that he may guide us to use it in his ways and for his purposes." Events in Guatemala offer another hideous example. When General Efraín Ríos Montt came to power in March of 1982, he presented himself as an ardent follower of Jesus. Seven months later, twenty-six hundred Guatemalan peasants — men, women, and children — had been killed. We cannot assume that those who dropped the bomb or murdered innocent Indians were psychopaths. Most of them were normal men born and raised in Christian families. They had been brought up to believe that what they were doing was a holy duty in the service of their country, a task of obedience to their God-fearing president, and even a mission given them by God.

Thus we come to the painful realization that our so-called good works and the works of those who drop bombs and commit genocide are not necessarily opposites. They might all have a place on the large spectrum of evil. Our wounds and needs and those of the men who dropped the bomb on Hiroshima and killed and tortured in Guatemala are not as different as we might like to think. The wounds and needs that lie behind the wars we condemn are the wounds and needs we share with the whole human race. We too are deeply marked by the dark forces that make one war emerge after another. We too are part of the evil we protest against.

Here we catch a glimpse of the true sinfulness of our humanity. It is a sin so deeply anchored in us that it pervades all of our lives. And when it is possible for "normal" human beings of our time to kill men, women, and children indiscriminately, why then would it not be possible for us to become accomplices in a worldwide mass murder in which the incineration of millions of people is considered acceptable? We too act in "obedience" and claim that what we do is in defense of our Christian values.

What then is the dwelling place of those who hate peace? It is our own familiar world in which peace is still ridiculed and in which the interlocking wounds and needs of individuals, groups, and nations continue to make war a more likely choice than peace.

Against this dark and fearful background I want to express the urgency of prayer as the first characteristic of the work of peacemaking.

The New Language

The invitation to a life of prayer is the invitation to live in the midst of this world without being dropped in the net of its wounds and needs. The word "prayer" stands for a radical interruption of the vicious chain of interlocking dependencies that lead to violence and war and for an entering into an entirely new dwelling place. It points to a new way of speaking, of breathing, of being together, of knowing — truly, to a whole new way of living.

It is not easy to express the radical change that prayer represents, since for many the word "prayer" is associated with piety: talking to God, thinking about God, attending morning and evening worship, going to Sunday service, saying grace before meals, and many other things. All of these have something to do with prayer, but when I speak about prayer as the basis for peacemaking I speak first of all about moving away from "the dwelling place of those who hate peace" into the house of God. Prayer is the center of the Christian life. It is the only necessary thing (Luke 10:42). It is living with God, here and now.

As I read the Gospels I am struck by how often images connected with a new dwelling place are used. These images bring me to think of the peacemaker as one who has found a new home where peace resides and from which peace is brought into the world. John the Evangelist describes Jesus as the Word of God who came into the world and pitched his tent among us (John 1:14). He also tells us how the first disciples asked Jesus when they first met him, "Teacher, where do you live?" and were invited to stay in this home (John 1:38–39). Here we are already made aware that following Jesus means changing places, entering into a new milieu and living in new company. The full meaning of this gradually unfolds in the Gospels. We come to see that Jesus not only invites his followers to live with him in the same house, but that he himself is the house.

On the evening before his death he says to his friends, "Make your home in me, as I make mine in you.... Whoever remains in me, with me in him, bears fruit in plenty" (John 15:4–5). This divine dwelling place enables us to live as peacemakers in a hostile world like sheep among wolves. In his words of farewell Jesus leaves no doubt about the nature of the world his followers have to live in, but he also assures them that they can live in the world with peace.

They will expel you from places of worship, and indeed the hour is coming when anyone who kills you will think he is doing a holy duty for God. They will do these things because they have never known either the Father or myself.... But I have told you all this so that you may find peace in me. In the world you will have trouble, but be brave: I have conquered the world. (John 16:2–3, 33)

These words powerfully express how prayer is the basis and the core of peacemaking. Even while being surrounded with conflict, wars, torture, and death, while being threatened by individual and collective destruction, we are not obliged to live in the dwelling place of those who hate peace. Prayer is the new language that belongs to the new house.

I would like to explore in some more detail what these biblical images of a new dwelling place can say to us who live in a world threatened by total extinction. It is not hard to see that the house of those who are for fighting is a house ruled by fear. One of the most impressive characteristics of Jesus' description of the end-time is the paralyzing fear that will make people senseless, causing them to run in all directions, so disoriented that they are swallowed up by the chaos that surrounds them. "There will be signs in the sun and moon and stars; on earth nations in agony bewildered by the clamor of the ocean and its waves; people dying of fear as they await what menaces the world, for the power of heaven will be shaken" (Luke 21:25–26). The advice that Jesus gives his followers for these times of turmoil is to remain quiet, confident, peaceful, and trusting in God. He tells them not to follow those who sow panic, nor to join those who claim to be saviors, nor to be frightened by rumors of wars and revolution, but "to stand erect and hold your heads high" (Luke 21:28).

Panic, fear, and anxiety are not part of peacemaking. This might seem obvious, but many who struggle against the threat of a world war not only are themselves motivated by fear but also use fear to bring others to action. Fear is the most tempting force in peacemaking. The stories about the arms race and descriptions of what would happen if a nuclear war were to take place are so terrifying that we are easily inclined to use that fear to bring ourselves as well as others to be advocates of peace. Many films, slide shows, and picture books are made with the explicit intention of shocking people into a change of mind and heart. We need to be reminded in very concrete ways of the demonic power at work in our world, but when an increase of fear is the main result we become the easy victims of these same powers. When peacemaking is based on fear it is not much different from warmaking. Although peacemakers may use words that are different from those used by warmakers, they still may be speaking the same language. They remain captive to the strategies of those who want to fight.

Peacemaking is the work of love, and "in love there can be no fear, but fear is driven out by perfect love" (1 John 18). Nothing is more important in peacemaking than that it flow from a deep and undeniable experience of love. Only those who deeply know that they are loved and rejoice in that love can be true peacemakers. Why? Because the intimate knowledge of being loved sets us free to look beyond the boundaries of death and to speak and act fearlessly for peace. Prayer is the way to that experience of love.

Prayer means entering into communion with the One who loved us before we could love. It is this "first love" (1 John 4:19) that is revealed to us in prayer. The deeper we enter into the house of God, the house whose language is prayer, the less dependent we are on the blame or praise of those who surround us, and the freer we are to let our whole being be filled with that first love. As long as we are still wondering what other people say or think about us and trying to act in ways that will elicit a positive response, we are still victimized and imprisoned by the dark world in which we live. In that dark world we have to let our surroundings tell us what we are worth. It is the world of successes and failures, of trophies and expulsions, of praise and blame, of stars and underdogs. In this world we are easily hurt and we easily act out of these hurts to find some satisfaction of our need to be considered worthwhile. As long as we are in the clutches of that world, we live in darkness, since we do not know our true self. We cling to our false self in the hope that maybe more success, more praise, more satisfaction will give us the experience of being loved, which we crave. That is the fertile ground of bitterness, greed, violence, and war.

In prayer, however, again and again we discover that the love we are looking for has already been given to us and that we can come to the experience of that love. Prayer is entering into communion with the One who molded our being in our mother's womb with love and only love. There, in that first love, lies our true self, a self not made up of the rejections and acceptances of those with whom we live, but solidly rooted in the One who called us into existence. In the house of God we were created. To that house we are called to return. Prayer is the act of returning.

Prayer is the basis of all peacemaking precisely because in prayer we come to the realization that we do not belong to the world in which conflicts and wars take place, but to him who offers us his peace. The paradox of peacemaking is indeed that we can speak of peace in this world only when our sense of who we are is not anchored in the world. We can say, "We are for peace," only when those who are for fighting have no power over us. We can bear witness for the Prince of Peace only when our trust is in him and him alone. In short, we can be in this world only when we no longer belong to it. This moving out of the world of warmakers in order to be in it as peacemakers is the Way of the Cross, which Jesus shows us. It is the long process of conversion in which we die to our old identity that is rooted in the ups and downs of worldly praise for all we do in the service of peace. Only by living in the house of peace can we come to know what peacemaking will mean.

This might sound very remote from the concrete down-to-earth daily problems we have to deal with. But the opposite is true. Only by opening ourselves to the language and way of prayer can we cope with the interruptions, demands, and ordinary tasks of life without becoming fragmented and resentful. Prayer — living in the presence of God — is the most radical peace action we can imagine.

The Act of Prayer

Most people think of prayer in contrast to action. They say or think: "Maybe prayer can prepare for action, maybe it can offer the right context for action, maybe it can be a way of expressing thanks for a successful action, but prayer itself is something different from action." This kind of thinking is built on the conviction that in prayer nothing much really happens and therefore prayer at best is of secondary importance, if not a complete waste of time and an evasion of reality. But if we are willing to see prayer as belonging to the essence of peacemaking and to consider the possibility that prayer itself *is* peacemaking and not simply the preparation before, the support during, and the thanksgiving after, we will have to struggle hard against the secular "dogma" of pragmatism. This is a crucial struggle, because it opens a new way of thinking that is especially important in a time when the nuclear threat makes peacemaking such an urgent necessity. Awareness of such urgency can easily lead us to a desperation that says: "There is now really no time for prayer; we need to act." But such an attitude contrasts sharply with Jesus' advice: "Stay awake, praying at all times for the strength to survive all that is going to happen, and to stand with confidence before the Son of Man" (Luke 21:36).

If we can come to the realization that it is in and through prayer that we find our true self, we already have a glimpse of its peacemaking quality. When we pray, we break out of the prison of blame and praise and enter into the houses of God's love. In this sense prayer is an act of martyrdom: in prayer we die to the self-destroying world of wounds and needs and enter into the healing light of Christ.

I found a very moving example of the power of prayer as an act in the way Floris Bakels describes his experiences in German concentration camps. Bakels, a sophisticated and well-educated Dutch lawyer, simply states that prayer saved him not only spiritually, but also mentally and physically. Why? Because prayer for him was a process of death and rebirth that enabled him to live as a hopeful and caring person even though hundreds of people around him were dying from hunger and being tortured and executed.

Bakels had never considered himself religious. Yet to his own surprise he found himself responding to his dying friends by speaking to them about "God, Jesus, and the Gospel" and discovering a peace in himself and others that was not of this world. It was hard for Bakels to grasp fully what was happening to him. But thirty-four years later he writes:

> I had an idea...hard to articulate....Being born again presupposes also for me a dying, a dying however of the old man, the birth of a new man.... But this departure of the old man...was an ultimate

sorrow, a "sorrow towards God," a world sorrow, a sorrow for what is passing, for the vanishing world, for the letting go of all things. . . . I started to realize my strong attachment to this world, but to the degree that this process of detachment developed itself, my adoration of the . . . beauty of this world increased. It was heartrending, it was one great birth pang. What to do? What about love, the love for a woman, my wife, my family, the butterflies, the waters and the forests? . . . All the attractiveness of that great rich life on earth. . . . Was I too attached to it? Under the shimmering of eternity I started a new process, a laying down of the old man, a saying farewell, a departing, even an attempt to be no longer so attached to life itself . . . and then . . . a wanting to take up the new man, to be a quiet flame, a reaching upwards, forgetting my own miserable body, a wanting to come home to the Power out of which I was created . . . couldn't articulate it well . . . I only knew one thing to do: to surrender everything to Him.

Floris Bakels expresses here the core of prayer as an act. It is the act of dying and being born again, of leaving the familiar house and coming home to the Power out of which we are created. The concentration camps of the Second World War opened Bakels to this experience. Today, as our world is slowly becoming one enormous concentration camp, threatened by a new and even greater holocaust, such acts of prayer are more crucial than ever. By radically breaking through the boundaries between life and death, prayer makes us free to stand in the midst of this world without being overwhelmed by fear.

In a situation in which the world is threatened by annihilation, prayer does not mean much when we undertake it only as an attempt to influence God, or as a search for a spiritual fallout shelter, or as a source of consolation in stress-filled times. In the face of a nuclear holocaust prayer makes sense only when it is an act of stripping oneself of everything, even of our own lives, so as to be totally free to belong to God and God alone.

This explains why, although we often feel a real desire to pray, we experience at the same time a strong resistance. We want to move closer to God, the source and goal of all peace, but the closer we come to him, the more intimately and urgently we experience his demand to let go of the many familiar ways in which we organize our lives. Prayer is such a radical act because it asks us to criticize our whole way of being in the world, to lay down our old selves, and to accept our new self, which is Christ.

This is what Paul has in mind when he calls us to die with Christ so that we can live with Christ. It is to this experience of death and rebirth that Paul witnesses when he writes: "I live now not with my own life, but with the life of Christ who lives in me" (Gal. 2:20).

What has all this to do with actions to end the arms race? I think that the most powerful protest against destruction is the laying bare of the basis of all destructiveness: the illusion of control. In the final analysis, isn't the nuclear arms race built upon the conviction that we have to defend — at all costs — what we have, what we

do, and what we think? Isn't the possibility of destroying
the earth, its civilizations, and its peoples a result of the
conviction that we have to stay in control — at all costs —
of our own destiny?

In the act of prayer, we undermine this illusion of control by divesting ourselves of all false belongings and by
directing ourselves totally to the God who is the only one
to whom we belong. Prayer, therefore, is the act of dying
to all that we consider to be our own and of being born
to a new existence which is not of this world.

Prayer is indeed a death to the world so that we can
live for God.

The great mystery of prayer, however, is that even now
it leads us already into God's house and thus offers us an
anticipation of life in the divine Kingdom. Prayer lifts us
up into the timeless immortal life of God.

There the meaning of the act of prayer in the midst of a
world threatened by extinction becomes visible. By the act
of prayer we do not first of all protest against those whose
fears drive them to build nuclear warheads, missiles, and
submarines. By the act of prayer we do not primarily attempt to stop nuclear escalation and proliferation. By the
act of prayer we do not even try to change people's minds
and attitudes. All this is very important and much needed,
but prayer is not primarily a way to get something done.

No, prayer is that act by which we appropriate the
truth that we do not belong to this world with its warheads, missiles, and submarines; we have already died to
it so that not even a nuclear holocaust will be able to
destroy us. Prayer is the act in which we willingly live

through, in our own being, the ultimate consequences of nuclear destruction, and affirm in the midst of them that God is the God of the living and that no human power will ever be able to "unmake" God. In prayer we anticipate both our individual death and our collective death and proclaim that in God there is no death but only life. In prayer we undo the fear of death and therefore the basis of all human destruction.

Is this an escape? Are we running away from the very concrete issues that confront us? Are we "spiritualizing" the enormous problems facing us and thus betraying our time, so full of emergencies? This would be true if prayer became a way to avoid all concrete actions. But if prayer is a real act of death and rebirth, then it leads us right into the world where we must take action.

To the degree that we are dead to the world, we can live creatively in it. To the degree that we have divested ourselves of false belongings, we can live in the midst of turmoil and chaos. And to the degree that we are free of fear, we can move into the heart of danger.

Thus the act of prayer is the basis and source of all action. When our actions against the arms race are not based on the act of prayer, they easily become fearful, fanatical, bitter, and more an expression of survival instincts than of our faith in God.

When, however, our act of prayer remains the act from which all actions flow, we can be joyful even when our times are depressing, peaceful even when we are constantly tempted to despair. Then we can indeed say in the face of the overwhelming nuclear threat: "We are not afraid, because we have already died and the world no longer has power over us." Then we can fearlessly protest against all forms of human destruction and freely proclaim that the eternal, loving God is "not the God of the dead but of the living" (Matt. 22:32).

What is the concrete day-to-day implication of this view of prayer? It is that we often have to take time to pray, and recognize prayer as the first and foremost act of resistance against the arms race. By allowing ourselves quiet time with God we act on our faith that the peace we want to bring is not the work of our hand or the product of movements we join, but the gift of Christ. Entering the special solitude of prayer is a protest against a world of manipulation, competition, rivalry, suspicion, defensiveness, anger, hostility, mutual aggression, destruction and war. It is a witness to the all-embracing, all-healing power of God's love. By not acting under the pressures of those who live their lives as victims of a series of emergencies, but standing quietly "with confidence before the Son of Man" (Luke 21:36), we act for peace. It certainly is not an easy act, since nearly everyone around us opposes it. The predominant voice says: "Keep moving. Keep working. Keep pushing. Keep talking, writing, organizing....Be sure to get things done...and done as soon as possible." But this voice is not the voice of the Lord of peace. Every time Jesus appears to his friends he calms their hearts and minds saying: "Don't be afraid, don't be agitated, don't be so doubtful" (see Luke 24:38).

When we enter into solitude we will often hear these two voices — the voice of the world and the voice of the

Lord — pulling us in two contrary directions. But if we keep returning faithfully to the place of solitude, the voice of the Lord will gradually become stronger and we will come to know and understand with mind and heart the peace we are searching for.

What do we do in our solitude? The first answer is nothing. Just be present to the One who wants your attention and listen! It is precisely in this "useless" presence to God that we can gradually die to our illusions of power and control and give ear to the voice of love hidden in the center of our being.

But "doing nothing, being useless," is not as passive as it sounds. In fact it requires effort and great attentiveness. It calls us to an active listening, in which we make ourselves available to God's healing presence and can be made new. The way to develop this attentive listening will vary with different people, but it always includes some type of meditation on the scripture. By quietly reading the psalms, reflecting on a scripture passage, or simply repeating a short prayer, we will find that the restless voices of our demanding world lose some of their power. We will feel more and more that the solitude offers us a home where we can listen to our Lord, where we can find the strength to be obedient to God's Word, and in which we can act freely and courageously.

There are endless forms of prayer, both individual and communal, but if we truly want to die to the old war-making self and take up lodging in the house of peace, we must take a hidden meditative stand in the presence of God. This is truly the great spiritual challenge of the peacemaker.

With a Contrite Heart

By describing prayer as an act I have tried to reemphasize the direct connection between the inner and the outer work of peacemaking. Although the remark "Change the world, begin with yourself" has often been used to individualize or spiritualize the urgent task of bringing peace to our planet, it points to the undeniable truth that peace in the world cannot be made without peace in the heart.

This is beautifully illustrated by a little story found in the tales of the Desert Fathers.

There were three friends who were eager workers, and one of them chose to devote himself to making peace between people who were fighting in accordance with "Blessed are the peacemakers." The second chose to visit the sick. The third went off to live in tranquillity in the desert. The first toiled away at the quarrels of men, but could not resolve them all, and so he went to the one who was looking after the sick, and he found him flagging too, not succeeding in fulfilling the commandment. So the two of them agreed to go and visit the one who was living in the desert. They told him of their difficulties and asked him to tell them what he had been able to do. He was silent for a time, then he poured water into a bowl and said to them, "Look at the water." It was all turbulent. A little later he told them to look at it again, and see how the water had settled down. When they looked at it, they saw their own faces as in a mirror. Then he said to them, "In the same way a person who is living in the midst of people does not see his own sins because of all the disturbance, but if he becomes tranquil, especially in the desert, then he can see his own shortcomings." (Benedicta Ward, *The Wisdom of the Desert Fathers*)

This story leaves little doubt that tranquility of the heart is not a way to "feel good" while the world is ripped apart by violence and war, but a way to come in touch with our being part of the problem. Prayer leads to spiritual tranquility and spiritual tranquility leads us to the confession of our sins, the sins that lead to war. Making peace between people and visiting the sick are important, but doing these things without a repentant heart cannot bear fruit. When we can see our own sinful self in a tranquil mirror and confess that we too are warmakers, then we may be ready to start walking humbly on the road to peace.

II

RESISTANCE

When the Second World War came to an end, I was only thirteen years old. Although my parents had skillfully protected me and my brother from the horror of the Nazis in my native Holland, they couldn't prevent me from seeing how our Jewish neighbors were led away, and from hearing about concentration camps to which they were deported and from which they never returned. Only in the years after the war did I become aware of the demonic dimensions of the Jewish persecution and learn the word "holocaust." And now, forty years later, I often ask myself: "Why was there not a massive popular uprising? Why weren't there marches of thousands of people protesting the genocide that was taking place? Why did the millions of religious people not invade the camps and tear down the gas chambers and ovens that were being built to annihilate the Jewish people? Why did those who pray, sing hymns, and go the church not resist the powers of evil so visible in their own land?"

It is important to find answers for these questions. But today I am no longer a thirteen-year-old boy who does not fully understand what is going on. Today I am an adult living only a few miles from the place where the Trident submarine is being built, a weapon able to destroy in one second more people than were gassed in Nazi Germany during the long years of the Hitler regime. Today I am a well-informed person fully aware of the genocide in Guatemala and the murderous terror in El Salvador. Today I am a well-educated teacher who is able to show clearly and convincingly that the costly arms race between the superpowers means starvation for millions of people all over the globe. Today I am a Christian who has heard the words of Christ many times and knows that the God of Israel and Jesus Christ is the God of the living in whom there is no shadow of death.

Today I am asking myself the question: "Does my prayer, my communion with the God of life, become visible in acts of resistance against the power of death surrounding me? Or will those who are thirteen years old today raise the same question about me forty years from now that I am raising about the adult Christians of my youth?" I have to realize that my silence or apathy may make it impossible for anyone to raise any questions forty years from today. Because what is being prepared is not a holocaust to extinguish a whole people but a holocaust that puts an end to humanity itself. That will make not only giving answers but also raising questions a total impossibility.

These thoughts are constantly on my mind. These concerns keep me wondering how to be a peacemaker today and every day of my life. I will never be able to say: "I didn't know what was going on." I do know with frightening accuracy what will happen when nothing is done. Being a peacemaker today requires that my prayer becomes visible in concrete actions. Without such actions my prayer remains the pious expression of a fearful mind that has abdicated responsibility for the future.

I have been so personal about this because I feel that I am not alone in this struggle. As I travel through life from day to day, I meet so many fellow travelers who see what I see, hear what I hear, and read what I read, and who are torn in their innermost selves by the same concerns that have come to me during the last decades. Like me, they are tempted to say: "We can't do much else but pray because we have our jobs, our families, our social obligations, and there is just no time left to work for peace. You can only do so much, and you have to accept your limitations." But in the face of a nuclear holocaust that threatens the very existence of jobs, family, and social obligations, they, as well as I, know that these excuses are groundless. Peacemaking is not an option any longer. It is a holy obligation for all people whatever their professional or family situation. Peacemaking is a way of living that involves our whole being all the time.

The word that I want to make central in these reflections on the daily life of the peacemaker is the word "resistance." As peacemakers we must resist resolutely all the powers of war and destruction and proclaim that peace is the divine gift offered to all who affirm life.

Resistance means saying "No" to all the forces of death, wherever they may be and, as a corollary, saying "Yes" to all of life in whatever form we encounter it.

Saying "No"

A Holy Necessity

To work for peace is to work for life. But, more than ever before in history, we are surrounded by the powers of death. The rapidly escalating arms race has created a death-mood that pervades our thoughts and feelings in ways that we are only vaguely aware of. We try to live and work as if all is normal, but we hardly succeed in keeping the voice of death away from us. It is the voice that says: "Why work when all you create will soon be destroyed? Why study when you doubt that you ever will be able to use your gifts? Why bring forth children when you cannot promise them a future? Why write, make music, paint, dance, and celebrate when existence itself is in doubt?"

We know that in the case of a full-scale Russian nuclear attack, 140 million Americans will probably die within days and we know that a U.S. retaliatory attack would take the lives of at least 100 million Russians. The fact that we can even think about such an event already does great harm to our minds and hearts. That human beings are considering saving their lives by killing millions of their fellow human beings is so preposterous that the words "saving life" have lost their meaning.

One of the most tragic facts of our century is that the "No" against the nuclear arms race has been spoken so seldom, so softly, and by so few. As I try to explain to myself my own lack of resistance against these dark forces of evil, it strikes me that I have always thought of the United States as a land of refuge for those who are persecuted —

as the land of freedom, endless opportunity, democracy, and the land that came to the help of the victims of Nazism. Yes, as the land that liberated my own country. These perceptions are so strong that even after such sinister events as the assassinations of John F. Kennedy, Robert Kennedy, and Martin Luther King Jr., the misery of Vietnam, and the scandal of Watergate, I have kept thinking of the United States as a country in which such events are painful exceptions. While such events are signs of an increasing betrayal of the ideals this country proclaims, I still have a very hard time believing that anything similar to what happened during the Hitler years in Germany can possibly take place here. After all, the United States won a crusade against Nazi tyranny. How could such a tyranny move to this side of the ocean?

Yet many of my friends who have gone to prison for saying "No" to the rapidly escalating arms race that causes millions of people to spend their lives building destructive weapons and other millions to suffer starvation are slowly opening my eyes to another America that I do not really want to see, but that can no longer be ignored. It is the America that prepared itself for "first strike capability," the ability not simply to prevent a nuclear attack by the threat of counterattack, but the ability to strike first and thus kill before being killed.

These friends have reminded me that the plans to fight and win a nuclear war are so completely contrary to Jesus' commandment of love and his own disarmed death on the cross, that not saying "No" is a sign of faithlessness. They have made me see that those who prepare for the death of millions of people and are willing to start a nuclear war are doing nothing illegal, while those whose conscience calls them to symbolically hammer down these present-day Auschwitzes and Dachaus are put in prison as criminals.

It is very hard for me to convert my thoughts and feelings to such a degree that I am willing to defend those who "break the law" in order to proclaim the higher law — a commandment of love to which I have dedicated my life. But if I truly believe in Jesus Christ as the man of peace who did not choose to appeal to his Father "who would promptly send more than twelve legions of angels to his defense" (Matt. 26:53–54), but who chose to die on a cross in total disarmament, how can I not be a man of peace? How can I allow the power of death to destroy the physical and moral life of millions, now as well as in the future, while remaining a passive and thus guilty bystander? Nonresistance makes us accomplices of a nuclear holocaust.

An "Original" Situation

The nuclear threat has created a situation that humanity has never faced before. History is filled with violence, cruelties, and atrocities committed by people against other people. Cities, countries, and whole civilizations have been erased from this planet and millions of people have become the victim of hatred and revenge. But never before has it been possible for humanity to commit collective suicide, to destroy the whole planet and put an end to all of history. This awesome capability was not even within our reach during the Second World War. The bombing of Hiroshima and Nagasaki at the end of the war gave us an inkling of what a next war might look like. But a future world war cannot be compared with any previous war. It will be a war that not only ends all war but also all peace.

It is this totally "original" situation that makes a "No" to war a universal necessity. It can no longer be seen as a necessity for certain people at certain times. When the being or not-being of humanity itself is at stake, we cannot allow ourselves to be distracted by other urgencies. Because nuclear war threatens not just the lives of millions but also any future in which the dead can be remembered, this threat overarches all other threats as cause for resistance. The small groups of "disobedient" people who jump the fences of nuclear weapons facilities, climb on board nuclear submarines, or put their bodies in front of nuclear transports are trying to wake us up to a reality we continue to ignore or deny. Their small numbers should not mislead us.

Throughout history the truth has seldom been spoken by majorities. Statistics are not the way truth becomes known. The prophets of Israel, Jesus and his few disciples, and the small bands of holy men and women throughout history are there to make us wonder if "these crazy peaceniks" might after all not be as important for our conversion today as St. Francis and his followers were eight centuries ago. Their loud, clear, and often dramatic "No" has to make us wonder what kind of "No" *we* are called to speak.

The Intimate Power of Death

When I try to come to terms with the effect of the nuclear threat on me, I realize that it not only brought me face to face with a completely new — and original — situation, but also makes me see in a new way the old and all-pervasive fascination with death that is an integral part of our daily lives. The confrontation with universal death has forced me to wonder about the more subtle ways in which death has us in its grip.

The Trident submarine, whose missiles can destroy many cities and countless people in one attack, is indeed the most insidious death machine human beings have ever created. But if we start saying "No" to this monster of destruction made by human hands, don't we also have to say "No" to the much less spectacular ways in which we play our death games? We are not simply victims of the power of death, for we are making Trident submarines and other nuclear weapon systems. The powers of death are far more intimate and pervasive than we are willing to confess.

Our ability to entertain even the possibility of a nuclear war is part of a much wider and deeper domination by death. We will never become true peacemakers until we are willing to unmask these death forces wherever and whenever they operate. An honest "No" against the nuclear arms race requires a "No" to the death hidden in the smallest corners of our minds and hearts. Peace in the world and peace of heart can never be separated. We need not answer the question: "Which is more important, peace in your heart or peace in the world?" Nor should we be distracted by arguments as to whether peace starts within or without. Inner and outer peace must never be separated. Peace work is a spectrum stretching from the hidden corners of our innermost selves to the most complex international deliberations. Our resistance against the powers of death must therefore be as deep and wide as peace itself.

Entertainment with Death

Not long ago I visited an exclusive American prep school. Most of the boys and girls came from well-to-do families, most were well educated, and all of them were very bright. They were friendly, well-mannered, and ambitious; it was not hard for me to imagine many of them eventually holding important positions, driving big cars, and living in large homes.

One evening I joined these students in watching a movie in the school's auditorium. It was *The Blues Brothers*. I could not believe what I was seeing and hearing. The screen was filled with the wild destruction of supermarkets, houses, and cars, while the auditorium was filled with excited shouts coming from the mouths of these well-mannered, bright young people. While they were watching the total devastation of all the symbols of their own prosperous lives, they yelled and screamed as if their team had won a championship. As cars were being smashed, houses set on fire, and high-rises pulled down, my excited neighbor told me that this was one of the most expensive "funny" movies ever made. Millions of dollars had been spent to film a few hours of what I considered to be death. No human beings were killed. It was supposed to bring a good laugh. But nothing human beings made was left untouched by the destructive activities of *The Blues Brothers.*

What does it mean that ambitious young Americans are being entertained by millions of dollars worth of destruction in a world in which many people die from fear, lack of food, and ever-increasing violence? Are these the future leaders of a generation whose primary task is to prevent a nuclear war and stop the arms race?

I report this seemingly innocent event to point to the fact that much contemporary entertainment is designed to feed our fascination with violence and death. Long hours of our lives are spent filling our minds with images not only of disintegrating skyscrapers and cars, but also of shootings, torture scenes, and other manifestations of human violence. Once I met a Vietnam veteran on an airplane. He told me that as a youngster he had seen so many people being killed on TV that once he got to Vietnam it had been hard for him to believe that those whom *he* killed would not stand up again and act in the next program. Death had become an unreal act. Vietnam woke him up to the truth that death is real and final and very ugly.

When I am honest with myself I have to confess that I, too, am often seduced by the titillating power of death. I am fascinated by someone who walks a tightrope strung over a gaping abyss. I bite my nails in excitement when I see trapeze artists making somersaults without a safety net beneath them. I look with open eyes and mouth at stunt pilots, motorcyclists, and race car drivers who put their lives at risk in their desire to break a record or perform a dazzling feat. In this respect, I am little different from the thousands of Romans who were entertained by the death games of the gladiators, or from the crowds who in the past and even the present are attracted to places of public execution.

Any suggestion that these real or imagined death games are healthy ways to deal with our "death-instincts" or "aggressive fantasies" needs to be discarded as unfounded, unproved, or simply irresponsible. Acting out death wishes either in fact or in the imagination can never bring us any closer to peace, whether it is peace of heart or peace in our life together.

Deadly Judgments

Our preoccupation with death, however, goes far beyond real or imagined involvement in physical violence. We find ourselves involved over and over again in much less spectacular but not less destructive death games. During my visit to Nicaragua and my subsequent lectures and conversations in the United States about the Nicaraguan people, I became increasingly aware of how quick judgments and stereotypes can transform people and nations into distorted caricatures, thus offering a welcome excuse for destruction and war. By talking one-dimensionally about Nicaragua as a land of Marxist-Leninist ideology, totalitarianism, and atheism we create in our mind a monster that urgently needs to be attacked and destroyed. Whenever I spoke about the people of Nicaragua and their deep Christian faith, their struggles for some economic independence, their desire for better health care and education, and their hope that they might be left alone to determine their own future, I found myself confronted with these deadening stereotypes. People would say: "But shouldn't we be aware that Russia is trying to get a foothold there and that we are increasingly being threatened by the dark powers of Communism?" Such remarks made me see that long before we start a war, kill people, or destroy nations, we have already killed our enemies mentally, by making them into abstractions with which no real, intimate human relationship is possible. When men, women, and children who eat, drink, sleep, play, work, and love each other as we do have been perverted into an abstract Communist evil that we are called — by God — to destroy, then war has become inevitable.

The Nazis were able to make the concrete human beings we call Jews into abstractions. They made them into "the Jewish problem." And for abstract problems there are abstract solutions. The solution to the Jewish problem was the gas chamber. And on the way to the gas chamber, there were many stages of dehumanizing abstraction: isolation from non-Jews, labeling with yellow stars, and deportation to faraway concentration camps. Thus the Jew became less and less one-of-us and more and more the stranger, the xxx, and finally "the problem."

As I reflect on the horrors of the Second World War, I realize how much violence was mental before it was physical. Today, again, it seems that a similar process is taking place. We have "made up our mind" about the Nicaraguans, the Cubans, the Russians, and these abstract creations of the mind are the first products of the powers of death.

Saying "No" to death therefore starts much earlier than saying "No" to physical violence, whether in war or entertainment. It requires a deep commitment to the words of Jesus: "Do not judge" (Matt. 7:1). It requires a "No" to all the violence of heart and mind. I personally find it one of the most difficult disciplines to practice.

Constantly I find myself "making up my mind" about somebody else: "He cannot be taken seriously. She is really just asking for attention. They are rabble rousers who only want to cause trouble." These judgments are indeed a form of moral killing. I label my fellow human beings, categorize them, and put them at a safe distance from me. By judging others I take false burdens upon myself. By my judgments I divide my world into those who are good and those who are evil, and thus I play God. But everyone who plays God ends up acting like the demon.

Judging others implies that somehow we stand outside of the place where weak, broken, sinful human beings dwell. It is an arrogant and pretentious act that shows blindness not only toward others but also toward ourselves. Paul says it clearly: "No matter who you are, if you pass judgment you have no excuse. For in judging others you condemn yourself, since you behave no differently from those you judge. We know God condemns that sort of behavior impartially" (Rom. 2:1–2).

I am moved by the idea that a peacemaker never judges anybody — neither his neighbor close by nor his neighbor far away; neither her friend nor her enemy. It helps me to think about peacemakers as persons whose hearts are so anchored in God that they do not need to evaluate, criticize, or weigh the importance of others. They can see their neighbors — whether they are North Americans, Russians, Nicaraguans, Cubans, or South Africans — as fellow human beings, fellow sinners, fellow saints, men and women who need to be listened to, looked at, and cared for with the love of God and who need to be given the space to recognize that they belong to the same human family as we do.

I vividly remember encountering a man who never judged anyone. I was so used to being around people who are full of opinions about others and eager to share them that I felt somewhat lost in the beginning. What do you talk about when you have nobody to discuss or judge? But, discovering that he also did not judge me, I gradually came to experience a new inner freedom within myself. I realized that I had nothing to defend, nothing to hide, and that I could be myself in his presence without fear. Through this true peacemaker, a new level of conversation opened up, based not on competing or comparing but on celebrating together the love of the One who is "sent into the world not to judge the world, but so that through him the world might be saved" (John 3:17). Through this man I came to realize that for Jesus, to whom God has entrusted all judgment (see John 5:22) the other name of judgment is mercy.

This encounter continues to change my life. For a long time I had simply assumed that I needed to have my opinions about everyone and everything in order to participate in ordinary life. But this man made me see that I am allowed to live without the heavy burden of judging others and can be free to listen, look, care, and fearlessly receive the gifts offered to me. And the more I become free from the inner compulsion to make up my mind quickly about who the other "really" is, the more I feel part of the whole human family stretched out over our planet from east to west and from north to south. Indeed, saying "No" to the violence of judgments leads me into the nonviolence of peacemaking, which allows me to embrace all who share life with me as my brothers and sisters.

Spiritual Suicide

But there is more. As peacemakers we must have the courage to see the powers of death at work even in our innermost selves because we find these powers in the way we think and feel about ourselves. Yes, our most intimate inner thoughts can be tainted by death.

When I reflect on my own inner struggles I must confess that one of the hardest struggles is to accept myself, to affirm my own person as being loved, to celebrate my own being alive. Sometimes it seems that there are evil voices hidden deeply in my heart trying to convince me that I am worthless, useless, and even despicable. It might sound strange, but these dark inner voices are sometimes most powerful when family and friends, students and teachers, and supporters and sympathizers cover me with praise.

Precisely then there are these voices who say: "Yes, but they really do not know me, they really cannot see my inner ugliness. If they could know and see they would discover how impure and selfish I am, and they would withdraw their praise quickly." This self-loathing voice is probably one of the greatest enemies of the peace-maker. It is a voice that seduces us to commit spiritual suicide.

The central message of the Gospel is that God sent his beloved Son to forgive our sins and make us new people, able to live in this world without being paralyzed by self-rejection, remorse, and guilt. To accept that message in faith and truly believe that we are forgiven is probably one of the most challenging spiritual battles we have to face. Somehow we cannot let go of our self-rejections. Somehow we cling to our guilt, as if accepting forgiveness fully would call us to a new and ominous task we are afraid to accept. Resistance is an essential element of peacemaking, and the "No" of the resisters must go all the way to the inner reaches of their own hearts to confront the deadly powers of self-hate.

I often think that I am such a hesitant peacemaker because I still have not accepted myself as a forgiven person, a person who has nothing to fear and is truly free to speak the truth and proclaim the kingdom of peace. It sometimes seems to me that the demonic forces of evil and death want to seduce me into believing that I do not deserve the peace I am working for. I then become self-accusing, apologetic, and even self-defeating, always hesitant to claim the grace I have been given and say clearly: "As a forgiven person I call forth the peace which is the fruit of forgiveness!"

My own inner struggles are not just my own. I share them with millions of others. Underneath much self-assured behavior and material success, many people think little of themselves. They might not show it — since that is socially unacceptable — but they suffer from it no less. Feelings of depression, inner anxiety, a sense of spiritual lostness, and (most painfully) guilt over past failures and past successes are often constant companions of highly respected men and women. These feelings are like small rodents slowly eating up the foundations of our lives.

Personally I believe that the battle against these suicidal inner powers is harder than any other spiritual battle. If those who believe in Jesus Christ were able to believe fully that they are forgiven people, loved unconditionally, and called to proclaim peace in the name of the forgiving Lord, our planet would not be on the verge of self-destruction.

A Far and Deeply Reaching "No"

It might seem contrived to extend the "No" of the peace-makers against nuclear war to a "No" against violent public entertainment, destructive stereotyping, and even self-loathing. But when we are trying to develop a spirituality of peacemaking we cannot limit ourselves to one mode of resistance. All levels need to be considered, even when it might seem that we are stretching things too far. I am deeply convinced that we have to keep all these forms of resistance together as parts of the great work of resistance. Peace activists who are willing to risk their freedom to prevent a nuclear holocaust, but who at the same time feed their imagination with violent scenes, give bad names to their fellow human beings, or nurture an inner disgust for themselves cannot be witnesses to life for very long. Full spiritual resistance requires a "No" to death wherever it operates.

Wherever there is life there is movement and growth. Wherever life manifests itself we have to be prepared for surprises, unexpected changes, and constant renewal. Nothing alive is the same from moment to moment. To live is to face the unknown over and over again. Life requires trust. We never know exactly how we will feel, think, and behave next week, next year, or in a decade. Essential to living is trust in an unknown future that requires a surrender to the mystery of the unpredictable.

At such a time as ours, in which everything has become unhinged and there is little to hold on to, uncertainty has become so frightening that we are tempted to prefer the certainty of death over the uncertainty of life. It seems that many people say in words or actions: "It is better to be sure of your unhappiness than to be unsure of your happiness." Translated into different situations this reads: "It is better to have clear-cut enemies than to have to live with people of whose lasting friendship you cannot be sure"; or, "It is better to ask people to accept your weaknesses than to be constantly challenged to overcome then"; or, "It is better to be defined as a bad person than to have to be good in constantly changing circumstances." It is shocking to see how many people choose the certainty of misery in order not to have to deal with the uncertainty of joy. This is a choice for death, a choice that is increasingly attractive when the future no longer seems trustworthy.

As I reflect on my childhood experiences of fear, I remember a time in which I was tempted to fail even before I had seriously tried to succeed. Somewhere I was saying to myself: "Why not run back from the diving board and cry so that you can be sure of pity, since you are not so sure of praise." Such childhood memories offer me an image of the temptation that faces all of us on a worldwide scale. It is the temptation to choose the satisfaction of death when the satisfaction of life seems too precarious. When the future has become a dark, fearful unknown that repulses me more and more, isn't it then quite attractive to opt for the satisfactions that are available in the present, even when these satisfactions are very partial, ambiguous, and tainted with death?

The nuclear situation in which the future itself has become not only dark and fearful but also uncertain has made the temptation to indulge ourselves in brief pleasures of the present greater than ever. It is therefore quite possible that we will see an increasing death-oriented self-indulgence going hand-in-hand with increasing doubt about a livable future. Fascination with death and hedonism are intimately connected, because both lust and death keep our eyes away from the anxiety-provoking future and imprison us in the pleasurable certainties of the present moment.

Peacemaking requires clear resistance to death in all its manifestations. We cannot say "No" to nuclear death if we are not also saying "No" to the less visible but no less hideous forms of death, such as abortion and capital punishment. As peacemakers we have to face the intimate connection between the varied forms of our contemporary fascination with death and the deaths caused by a nuclear holocaust. By recognizing in our own daily lives our many "innocent" death games, we gradually come to realize that we are part of that complex network of warmaking that finds its most devastating expression in a nuclear holocaust.

Real resistance requires the humble confession that we are partners in the evil that we seek to resist. This is a very hard and seemingly endless discipline. The more we say "No," the more we will discover the all pervasive presence of death. The more we resist, the more we recognize how much more there is to resist. The world — and we are an intimate part of the world — is indeed Satan's territory. When the demon shows Jesus all the kingdoms of the world and their splendor he says: "I will give you all these, if you fall at my feet and worship me" (Matt. 4:9). Jesus never disputes that these kingdoms are Satan's; he only refuses to worship him. The world and its kingdoms are under the destructive power of the evil spirit, the spirit of destruction and death. The nuclear threat reveals the ultimate implication of this truth. It is not that God — who created the world out of love — will destroy it, but that *we* will destroy it when we allow the satanic power of death to rule us. This is what makes saying "No" to death in all its manifestations such an urgent spiritual task.

Saying "Yes"

Do Not Combat the Demons Directly

While discussing the "No" of resistance I already alluded to the "Yes" of resistance. It is clear that resisting the forces of death is meaningful only when we are fully in touch with the forces of life. What is finally important is not that we overcome death but that we celebrate life.

I have found that told concentration on fighting the forces of destruction is dangerous and can be very damaging. When I allow my mind and heart to experience what a nuclear holocaust will do to our planet, it often seems that a deep darkness starts to surround me and pull me into a pit of depression and despair. When I try to confront the powers of death that already have a hold on me, I often feel so powerless that I lose contact with the source of my own life. How easy it is to become a victim of the very forces I am fighting against! When all my attention goes to protesting death, death itself may end up receiving more attention than it deserves. Thus my struggle against the dark forces of death becomes the arena of my own seduction. I often wonder if my own depression and the depression of many of my friends is not an ominous sign that our many attempts to say "No" have already harmed us more than we are willing to confess.

There is a very old piece of wisdom that comes from the fourth-century monks of the Egyptian desert: "Do not combat the demons directly." The desert fathers felt that a direct confrontation with the forces of evil required so much spiritual maturity and saintliness that few would be ready for it. Instead of paying so much attention to the prince of darkness, they advised their disciples to focus on the Lord of light and thus, indirectly but inevitably, undo the power of the demon. The desert fathers thought that a direct confrontation with the demon would give the demon precisely the attention he is trying to get. Once he has our attention he has the chance to seduce us. That is the story of the fall. Eve's first mistake was to listen to the serpent and consider him worthy of response. Once Satan had her attention it was not hard for him to make her eat the forbidden fruit.

This early Christian wisdom is very important for peacemaking. As a peacemaker, my temptation is to underestimate the power of the forces of death and thus attack them directly. Precisely because I am such a sinful, broken person, these forces have many handles on me and can easily entangle me in their network. Only the sinless Christ was able to overcome death. It is naïve to think that we have the strength to face death alone and survive.

Here we touch one of the greatest dangers that face peacemakers: that peacemakers themselves become the victims of the evil forces they are trying to overcome. The same fear of "the enemy" that leads warmakers to war can begin to affect the peacemaker who sees the warmaker as "the enemy." Words of anger and hostility can gradually enter into the language of the peacemaker. Even the sense of urgency and emergency that motivates the arms race can become the driving force behind the peacemaker. Then indeed the strategy of war and the strategy of peace have become the same, and peacemaking has lost its heart. This is far from a theoretical possibility. When I become grim, resentful, and angry, when my heart is preoccupied with schemes to manipulate people into my camp, and when I no longer radiate any of the peace I am trying to make visible in the world, how can I expect to convince, attract, or motivate anybody else to become a peacemaker?

One of the reasons that so many people have developed strong reservations about the peace movement is precisely that they do not see the peace they seek in the peacemakers themselves. Often what they see are fearful and angry people trying to convince others of the urgency of their protest. Thus the tragedy is that peacemakers often reveal more of the demons they are fighting than of the peace they want to bring about.

Love Your Enemy

The words of Jesus go right to the heart of our struggle; "Love your enemy, do good to those who hate you, bless those who curse you, pray for those who treat you badly" (Luke 6:27–28). The more I reflect on these words, the more I consider them to be the test for peacemakers. What my enemies deserve is not my anger, rejection, resentment, or disdain, but my love. Spiritual guides throughout history have said that love for the enemy is the cornerstone of the message of Jesus and the core of holiness.

For us fearful people, loving our enemy is the greatest challenge, because our fears make us divide the world between people who are for us and people who are against us, people to love and people to hate, friends and enemies. All these distinctions are based on the illusion that our fellow human beings decide who we are and that our very being depends on their words, thoughts, and actions. Loving our enemy thus compels us to unmask this illusion by acting according to the knowledge that God loves all human persons — regardless of their sex, religion, race, color, nationality, age, or intelligence — with the same bold, unconditional love. The distinction between friends and enemies is made by us fearful people, not by our loving God. Therefore it is essential for peacemakers to be deeply rooted in this all-embracing love of God, who "causes the sun to rise on the bad as well as the good, and the rain to fall on honest and dishonest people alike" (Matt. 5:45). It is only this deep rootedness in God's all-inclusive love that can prevent the peacemaker from being ravaged by the same anger, resentment, and violence that leads to war.

What has all this to do with the work of resistance? It means that only a loving heart, a heart that continues to affirm life at all times and places, can say "No" to death without being corrupted by it. A heart that loves friends and enemies is a heart that calls forth life and lifts up life to be celebrated. It is a heart that refuses to dwell in death because it is always enchanted with the abundance of life. Indeed, only in the context of this strong loving "Yes" to life can the power of death be overcome. I therefore want to say here as clearly as I can that the first and foremost task of the peacemaker is not to fight death but to call forth, affirm, and nurture the signs of life wherever they become manifest.

The Search for the Tender and Vulnerable Life

Death is solid, uniform, unchangeable. It is also big, boisterous, noisy, and very pompous. A military parade, in which tanks and missiles are proudly displayed, preceded and followed by disciplined, uniformed soldiers, is a typical manifestation of the death force. Life is different. Life is very vulnerable. Life, when first seen, needs protection — a plant slowly opening its flowers, a bird trying to leave its nest, a little baby making its first noises. It is very small, very hidden, very fragile. Life does not push itself to the foreground. It wants to remain hidden and only hesitantly reaches out. Life is soft-spoken. The sounds of life come gently and often seem part of the silence in which they are heard. Life moves moderately: no quick, brisk steps but a growth so imperceptible that we never really see it, only recognize it. Life touches gently. It does not slap or beat, but caresses and strokes. It makes us speak a tender language: "Be still, she is asleep." And then later: "You can come now and look. Isn't she beautiful? Do you want to hold her for a moment? Be careful."

Those who resist the power of death are called to search for life always and everywhere. The search for this tender and vulnerable life is the mark of the true resister. I have learned this from friends who have dedicated themselves to resistance. They have helped me to appreciate

anew the beauty of life. One of them spends an afternoon every week visiting cancer patients, another works
with the mentally disabled, a third spends time with lonely
people in a psychiatric institution. Somehow their direct
contact with the powers of death has made them aware of
the preciousness of life and given them the desire to affirm
life precisely where it is weak and very tender. Their quiet
and unspectacular care for broken people has become for
them a true form of resistance.

Not Quenching the Wavering Flame

This has opened my eyes to life in a new way. Having a
baby seems such a natural, obvious, and rather unspectacular event. But for those who are deeply aware that
we are living on a planet that is being prepared for total
destruction, in a time that can be sure only of the past
and the present but not of the future, giving life to a new
human being becomes an act of resistance. Bringing into
the world a little child totally dependent on the care of
others and leading it gradually to maturity is true defiance
of the power of death and darkness. It is saying loudly:
For us life is stronger than death, love is stronger than
fear, and hope is stronger than despair.

I still remember vividly how my friend Dean Hammer
spoke about the baby he and his wife, Katie, were expect-
ing. Dean had just spent several months in prison for civil
disobedience for a "Plowshares" disarmament action and
was facing the possibility of another sentence that might
put him behind bars for several years. But in the midst
of all the worries about their personal future as well as

their deep concern for the future of the world, waiting for this baby felt to them like another type of disobedience, a disobedience of the powers that could only give birth to death. When Hannah was born, she was received as a sign of the divine victory of life over death.

Having known Dean and Katie for many years, and having followed their agonizing struggle against the nuclear arms race, I was able to see Hannah in ways I had never seen a baby before. This small and fragile new child, looking trustfully at me with her beautiful dark eyes, told me something new about resistance that I had not known before. She told me that there is hope even when optimism seems absurd: there is love even when people die of fear; and there is reason to celebrate even in a civilization dressed in mourning for its own rapid decline.

When I held little Hannah and saw the intense joy of Dean and Katie, I knew that the "No" to death that had led Dean to go to prison was such a hopeful "No" because it was undergirded by a strong and fearless "Yes" to life. And with little Hannah in my arms, I could easily make the connections between resisting nuclear weapons and protecting the unborn child, caring for the severely mentally and physically disabled, offering support to the elderly, defending the life of the prisoners on death row, and reaching out to all people whose life is precarious. The Lord of life is the Lord who does not "break the crushed reed, nor quench the wavering flame" (Isa. 42:3). In our utilitarian, pragmatic, and increasingly opportunistic society, however, there is less and less room for the weak, the prisoners, the broken, and the dying. The crushed reed is easily discarded and the wavering flame easily quenched.

Reflecting on the affirmation of life as an act of resistance, I gradually came to see three aspects of life which are in stark contrast to the powers of death. They are humility, compassion, and joy. These three aspects of life therefore must also characterize the "Yes" of the resister. I would like to explore a little more now how a humble, compassionate, and joyful "Yes" is the way to true peace.

A Humble "Yes"

The peacemaker's "Yes" to life is first of all a humble "Yes." The world "humble" comes from the Latin word *humus,* which means soil. Humble people are close to the soil and thus able to see and experience their lives as deeply connected with all other lives. If I learned anything during my visits to Latin America it was the humility of the poor. Their humility had nothing to do with self-deprecation or self-refection, but everything to do with their connectedness with the land and the people. In our modern civilization, so much emphasis is placed on being different, unique, and special, that it is very hard to remain truly connected. For us the most important question is: "How am I distinct from others?" This question often makes us lose sight of our basic sameness as created human beings. Humility is the joyful recognition that we belong to the created world, that we are fellow human beings, and that we are intimately connected with all that lives and moves. As long as our distinctiveness is our major concern, we put ourselves on the dangerous road

of comparing and competing. When countries and con-
tinents follow this road, violence, war, and even global
suicide are real possibilities. But when we are willing to
acknowledge and even celebrate our intimate connectedness as human beings we are on the road to peace. Being
older or younger, smarter or more attractive, stranger or
friend, Russian or American becomes less important than
being a member of the human family. It is the freeing affirmation: "I am like all other people and I am grateful
for it!"

It is important that the peacemaker's "Yes" be a humble
"Yes." It is humility that allows us to consider a quiet
afternoon with a distressed friend just as important as
any spectacular peace action. Visible and publicized peace
actions are important to raise people's awareness of the
sinister consequences of human arrogance and pride, but
"passing" an afternoon with a friend in pain is a humble
celebration of our common humanity. Such a simple act
is indeed like the sowing of a mustard seed.

Visiting the sick, feeding the hungry, consoling the
dying, or sheltering the homeless may not catch the public eye and are often perceived as irrelevant when put in
the perspective of a possible nuclear holocaust. There are
many voices who say: "These little acts of mercy are a
waste of time when we consider the urgency of stopping
the arms race." But the peacemaker knows that true peace
is a divine gift which has nothing to do with statistics
or measures of success and popularity. Peace is like life
itself. It manifests itself quietly and gently. Who can say
that a "lost afternoon" with a sick friend is in truth not

much more than an interruption of "true" peacework? It might be the most real contribution to peace. Who knows? Jesus' way is the humble way. He calls out to us: "Learn from me for I am gentle and humble of heart" (Matt. 11:29). A humble "Yes" to all forms of life — even the less noticed — affirms the deep interconnection between all people and forms the true basis of peace.

A Compassionate "Yes"

The peacemaker's "Yes" also has to be a very compassionate "Yes," a "Yes" that constantly keeps the concrete, unique suffering of individual people in mind. During the past few years I have become increasingly aware of the temptation to focus more on issues than on people. But when our peace work is primarily issue-oriented it easily loses heart and becomes cold, calculating, and very impersonal. When we fight for issues and no longer see concrete people with their unique personalities and histories, competition will dominate compassion and winning the issue may mean losing the people. There are endless problems in the world — poverty, oppression, exploitation, corruption — that urgently beg for solutions. But people are not problems. They smile and cry, work and play, struggle and celebrate. They have names and faces to be remembered.

When I went to Peru for the first time I was strongly motivated by the burning issues of Latin America. I had heard and read about illiteracy, malnutrition, poor health, infant mortality, and many other problems. I was so overwhelmed by my own privileged position that I could no longer tolerate my "splendid isolation" and wanted to do something to alleviate the suffering of my fellow human beings. But when I arrived in to Peru and began living there, what I came to know first of all were not issues but people: Sofía, who struggled with back pain; Pablo, who lost his job over and over again; María, who dreamed about having her own doll; Pablito, who wanted to go to the library and read books; and Juanito, who loved playing practical jokes on me. They certainly suffered from poverty, oppression, and exploitation, but what they asked of me more than anything was not to solve their many problems, but to become their friend, share my life with them, mourn with them in their sadness, and celebrate with them in their gladness.

When our "Yes" remains compassionate, that is, people-oriented, the complex issues of our time will not drag us down into despair and our hearts will burn with love. We cannot love issues, but we can love people, and the love of people reveals to us the way to deal with issues. A compassionate resister always looks straight into the eyes of real people and overcomes the human inclination to diagnose the "real problem" too soon.

There is no question about the need for critical analysis of the world we live in. We have to try constantly to identify the main dynamics that create poverty, hunger, homelessness, oppression, and war. Helping individual people in need is not the final answer. But when we become so overwhelmed by the abstract problem that we no longer consider the concrete, daily pain of men, women, and children worthy of our attention, we have already been seduced by the demon of death. Jesus understood the problems of the world in the most radical way, but wherever he went he responded to the concrete needs of people. A blind man saw again; a sick woman was healed; a mother saw her dead son come back to life; an embarrassed wedding host was given the wine he needed; thousands of hungry people received bread and fish to eat. Jesus left no doubt that the help he offered was only a sign of a much greater renewal. However, he never let that truth prevent him from responding to the concrete and immediate concerns of the people he met.

A Joyful "Yes"

Finally, the peacemaker's "Yes" is a joy-filled "Yes." The fruit of humility and compassion is joy. When we resist the powers of death and destruction with a sad heart we cannot bring peace. Joy is one of the most convincing signs that we work in thc Spirit of Jesus. Jesus always promises joy; a joy like the joy of a mother after childbirth (see John 17:21); a joy that no one can take from us (see John 16:22); a joy that is not of this world but a participation in the divine joy, a joy that is complete (see John 15:11). There probably is no surer sign of a true peacemaker than joy.

Sadness, bitterness, anger, and melancholy are dark experiences that show how close to the powers of death we have come. Where there is joy there is life. When Elizabeth heard the greeting of her cousin Mary, the child in her womb leapt for joy (see Luke 1:44). New life always leaps for joy — parents welcoming a child, children discovering the world, young people falling in love, men and women standing in admiration of the beauty of nature. Joy is a free leaping toward the unexpected, a lifting up of what is new, a reaching out to heaven in hope, a touching of the Kingdom, an expectant tiptoeing. Sadness is always stagnant, heavy, and old. There is no old joy. Joy is always moving, light, and new.

Affirming life always brings joy. I have been amazed by the joy that radiates from the faces of those who work with the poorest of the poor. When I first saw the miserable and seemingly hopeless conditions in which many of these men and women have to live and work, I expected depression and despair. But what I found among the most committed was joy. While teaching little children to read and write, feeding the hungry, visiting the sick, and caring for the dying, they spoke to me about the immense joy that had grown in their hearts. Some would say: "I love to be here with these poor people. Here I come to know Jesus and he has given me joy I never knew before."

When I heard these words for the first time, I felt a deep jealousy. I wanted that joy so much for myself but had not found it among the scholars, teachers, and students with whom I spend most of my time. I was suddenly struck by how somber and sad my friends and I are. We have enough food and shelter and more than enough health care and education, but are we living joyful lives? Why are we so serious all the time, so intense, so preoccupied with the next thing to accomplish, so disappointed after a small setback, so apprehensive when we are not being noticed, so angry when we are rejected, and so deeply sad when life is not going as we had planned it? When we are entangled in many complex issues, sadness can indeed imprison us and take away from us the joy we so much desire.

Many peacemakers, overwhelmed by the great threats of our time, have lost their joy and have become prophets of doom. Yet anyone who grimly announces the end of the world and then hopes to move people to peace work is not a peacemaker. Peace and joy are like brother and sister; they belong together. I cannot remember a moment of peace in my life that wasn't also very joyful. In the Gospels, joy and peace are always found together. The angel who announces the birth of Christ, the prince of peace, to the shepherds says: "Listen, I bring you news of great joy to be shared with the whole people" (Luke 2:10). And when Jesus has completed his work of peace on earth and is lifted up to heaven, the disciples return to Jerusalem "full of joy" (Luke 24:52). Thus the Gospel of peace is also a Gospel of joy. Thus, peace work is joyful work.

This joy does not necessarily mean happiness. In the world we are made to believe that joy and sorrow are opposites and that joy excludes pain, suffering, anguish, and distress. But the joy of the Gospel is a joy born on the cross. It is not the sterile happiness of victory parties, but the deep joy that is hidden in the midst of the struggle. It is the joy of knowing that evil and death have no final power over us, a joy anchored in the words of Jesus: "In the world you will have trouble, but be of good cheer; I have conquered the world" (John 16:33).

Resist — Solid in Your Faith

Thus the "No" to death can be fruitful only when spoken and acted out in the context of a humble, compassionate, and joyful "Yes" to life. Resistance becomes a truly spiritual task only when the "No" to death and the "Yes" to life are never separated.

Increasing starvation, hunger, and poverty around the world and the increasing threat of a nuclear war offer us many reasons to be fearful, even despairing. When we hear the voices of death all around us and see so many signs of the superiority of the powers of death, it becomes hard to believe that life is indeed stronger than death. Long before anyone knew about nuclear war, Peter warned his people: "Your opponent the devil is prowling like a roaring lion looking for someone to devour" (1 Pet. 15:8). These words have a new and concrete relevance for us. They summarize well our fear. It is indeed the fear of a roaring lion ready to attack us and tear us to pieces.

What is Peter's response to this lion? "Resist him," he says, "solid in faith" (1 Pet. 5:9). And that indeed is the summary of the spiritual response to any threat. It is faithful resistance, a resistance based not on our experience, skills, intelligence, or willpower, but on our faith in Christ who has already overcome the powers of evil and death that rule the world. Through Christ's victory over all death, individual as well as collective, death has no final power over us any longer. We are no longer locked in the dark world of despair but have already found our home in God where death has no place and life is everlasting.

Though we are still in this world, we no longer belong to it. Our faith allows us even now to be members of God's household, and taste even now the inexhaustible love of God. It is this knowledge of where we truly belong that sets us free to be fierce resisters against death while humbly, compassionately, and joyfully proclaiming life wherever we go.

RESISTANCE AS PRAYER

Where Do We Pray?

Having explored the "No" and the "Yes" of resistance I am now left with the task of explaining that resistance does not stand in contrast to prayer, but is in fact a form of prayer itself. It is hard to overcome our tendency to consider resistance as the active part of peacemaking and prayer as its contemplative part. But I am increasingly convinced that we will fully grasp the meaning of peacemaking only when we recognize not only that prayer is a form of resistance but also that resistance is a form of prayer.

It has taken me many years to understand this fully. The reason for my not understanding this sooner is probably that I had stayed away from most public forms of resistance and even had for a long time a deep resistance against resistance. Every time I saw people demonstrating against nuclear war in front of an office building or industrial plant, I experienced some inner irritation. I often rationalized this irritation by thinking about the demonstrators as angry people who had nothing else to do. I was also convinced that these small bands of poorly dressed sign carriers were totally ineffectual, not only unable to change anything but also making things worse for those who want to work for peace through normal means.

But when friends invited me to come closer and watch more attentively, I gradually came to realize that I might have been turned off as much by Jesus and his disciples as by these small groups of resisters. What they did, said, and enacted referred to a reality with which we have lost contact. It is the reality of God's forgiveness and love by which divisions among people are removed and unity is restored. What I had been talking about in pulpits and writing about in books was given direct, concrete visibility by these "street people." What seemed totally acceptable to everybody when surrounded by a nice ceremony on a Sunday morning suddenly seemed useless, exaggerated, and irritating when acted out in front of a nuclear facility. The closer I came to my resisting friends, the more I realized that they were doing no less and no more than witnessing for the God of the living in a place where the powers of death are most clearly at work.

Then, one year, during Holy Week, a small group of theology students invited me to join them in a prayer vigil at Electric Boat, the nuclear submarine shipyard in Groton, Connecticut. I knew these students to be hard-working, intelligent, and deeply believing men and women. Their invitation was sincere, personal, and based on their knowledge of my own convictions. I realized that I was asked little more than to proclaim the Word of God at a place where it would clearly be heard as confronting the powers of death and calling for conversion. Although I felt a certain fear of making a fool of myself, I knew that there was only one answer: "Yes."

On Holy Thursday we all gathered in preparation for this Good Friday peace action. The first thing I discovered was that this action group was indeed a prayer group. For many months these women and men had come together at least once a week to pray. During these times they had gradually grown into a community of people able to listen to God's guidance. Together they had read and studied the scriptures, spoken about their fears and apprehensions, tried to find words to express their deepest convictions. Together they had come to the decision that they should be willing to bring their prayers right to the place where their deepest fear found its cause: the place where the Trident Submarine was being built.

It had been a hard and slow spiritual journey for most of these theology students. Many of them came from traditional American families, in which respect for the authority of church and government goes hand in hand. Public protest against what the government considers necessary for the protection of the people would create deep indignation. And yet, quiet listening day after day and week after week to the Word of God while reading more and more about the final destruction that the Trident submarine can bring about had brought these men and women to a new clarity: "We have to say 'No' to what our government is doing in Groton." Some felt that they had to break the law and let themselves be arrested. Others were less clear about that. But everyone was united by the inner call to say "No" to death and "Yes" to the God of life in a way that was exceptional and visible enough for the world to respond.

What most impressed me was that these friends did not want to go to Groton to shake their fists at the warmakers and confront them with threats. If anything had emerged from their prayers it was that they themselves were the first who needed to be converted and that there was no basis whatsoever for self-righteousness. It was not "We," the good people, against "Them," the bad people. On the contrary, there was a deep awareness that those who work long days at Electric Boat are people caught in the same trap of warmaking as we are. They want to earn enough money to care for their families and educate their children. They work for their own dignity and self-respect. They work because they love their fellow human beings, their country, and their God. The unspeakable tragedy is that if the products of their hard work are ever used there will no longer be anyone to care for.

The more I listened to the students who had invited me to join them in their Good Friday peace action, the more it sounded like a pilgrimage of repentance, a witness to themselves as well as others, a call for conversion that includes first of all the one who makes the call. They reminded me of the prophet who responded to those who criticized his effectiveness with the words: "I do not preach against the evils of the world to just change the world, but to prevent the world from changing me."

The Stations of the Cross

On Good Friday we went to Groton to witness for peace in front of the administration building of Electric Boat. The leaders of the group asked me to lead the community in the Stations of the Cross. I couldn't resist a smile when I heard that we, people from very different denominations (Baptist, Presbyterian, Lutheran, United Church of Christ, and Catholic), would make the Stations of the Cross. As a child I had often made these fourteen stations in church. They commemorate fourteen events between Jesus' being condemned to death by Pontius Pilate and his burial. These events have been vividly portrayed in paintings and sculpture, and I remember well how my Dutch teenage friends and I walked from station to station in the chapel of our high school, not once in a while, but many times a week during our lunch breaks.

But as I grew older the Stations of the Cross soon became a pious childhood memory. The Second Vatican Council had so altered my religious consciousness that I, together with most of my fellow Catholics, dropped this devotional practice and focused on official liturgical celebration. Who could have dreamt that twenty years after the Council I would lead an ecumenical group of theology students in the Stations of the Cross on the streets of Groton, Connecticut, in prayerful resistance against an impending nuclear holocaust?

He Died for Those Who Prepare to Kill

As soon as we arrived at the site I put on my white alb and purple stole and followed the large wooden cross that the students had made for the ceremony. Fourteen students had been selected to reflect on the passion of Jesus at the different stations, and fourteen others to show how Jesus' passion spoke to the nuclear threat of today.

We prayed fervently with words and songs as well as in silence. We heard the story of Jesus suffering in a way we could not have heard it in any church. It was hard for me to know fully how I felt, but something new was happening to me that I had never experienced before. It was the deep awareness that prayer was no longer a neutral event without danger. Moreover, the words I had so often spoken about death and resurrection, about suffering and new life, suddenly received a new power, a power to condemn death unambiguously and call forth life.

Resistance Is Liturgy

I have told this personal story because it was my way of discovering that resistance is not action in contrast to prayer, but a true form of prayer. After my own, very limited, experience with war resistance I even dare to say that, for those who resist in the name of the living God, resistance is not only prayer but also liturgy. As I reflect more fully on my experience in Groton I have come to see that it can easily be seen and understood as a liturgical experience. The word "liturgy" comes from the Greek phrase *ergos to lao*, which means "the work of the people." It is the communal work of worship by the people of God.

My Good Friday experience at Groton is only one example of the many ways in which Christian resisters are reclaiming the peacemaking power of liturgical celebrations. Traditional feast days, such as the feast of the Holy Innocents on December 28, or the feast of the Transfiguration of Christ on August 6, can become radical calls to conversion for our age. For ours is an age in which children can be innocent victims of the nuclear bomb, and in which the deadening light of Hiroshima has replaced the life-giving light of Mount Tabor.

As the peace movement grows deeper and stronger, more holy days are becoming peacemaking days. The "Peace Pentecost" celebrated in the National Cathedral in Washington in 1983 and followed by a day of massive civil disobedience in the Capitol building is another example of "liturgical renewal." In such a liturgy the scriptures read, the hymns sung, and the gifts shared are transforming the conscience of the people and offering the strength for them to go and live out the peace of God, even when it leads to ridicule, rejection, and jail. As we see the liturgical year becoming a year of peacemaking we rediscover Advent, Christmas, Epiphany, Lent, Easter, Pentecost, and many other holy days and seasons as carrying within themselves a very specific message of peace. As we live under threat that this century could be the last century in history, the liturgical year must proclaim in all its celebrations the peace of Christ which is not of this world but was brought to this world for its salvation.

By our worship we create together the new heaven and the new earth, and lay the foundation for the Kingdom of God among us. By making ourselves vulnerable to God and to each other and sharing in a very simple way these signs of peace, we are building God's dwelling place right in the heart of this world. Thus we continue the incarnation of God's Word of peace and invite those who are living in darkness to enter with us into the house of God's love.

I have always believed this to be true, but when I saw and experienced this worship in front of the place where the instruments of death are being built, I came to understand how radical the peacework of God's people really is.

Not Based on Success

If I have created thus far the impression that the ideal form of peace work is a liturgy on the street, that would be the wrong impression. I simply wanted to explain through a concrete example that resistance is indeed a form of prayer and devotion. This for me is of crucial importance since so many resisters experience burnout when they realize that no significant change in the socioeconomic or political situation has been achieved. Many people who have worked very hard for years in the hope of bringing about change have finally given up in despair. When they realized that things had not gotten better, but worse, that political parties, corporations, and elected officers had not changed their ways, they withdrew into passive resignation, no longer believing it worthwhile to keep struggling.

But Christian resistance cannot be dependent on signs of success. It is first and foremost a spiritual resistance, based not on results but on its own inherent integrity. Once we have let go of the compulsions of our success-driven world and have entered into God's house of prayer and praise, our resistance can be free from the need to be "useful." Then our resistance can be a clear witness to the living God in the midst of a world obsessed with death. Whatever we do to resist the powers of death, it must first and foremost be an expression of worship of the living God.

When we see the behavior of many people in peace demonstrations we may be tempted to laugh at their "useless" activities. But when we come to see that these people are doing what they are doing first of all to be faithful to their God and to offer God praise at all times and at all places, we may come to see them as we see the three young men who refused to worship the golden statue that king Nebuchadnezzar had made and instead worshiped God in the fiery furnace (Daniel 3).

Indeed, more important than our effect on people is our own spiritual authenticity. If we want to be faithful to our new self, which we have received from our Lord Jesus Christ, then we cannot remain silent and passive in the presence of the mounting forces of death. We owe it to God and to ourselves to say "No," for the alternative, silence, means becoming an accomplice in war and thus losing the gift of peace that God has given us. Here we are touching the core of all resistance. It is an act flowing forth from our own deepest understanding of who we are. It is an act of spiritual integrity. It is a way of proclaiming the peace that we have found in God's house. It is an expression of what we have become through the transforming power of Jesus. In this sense, it is a true act of prayer. And true prayer does not calculate the consequences.

The Many Ways of Resistance

Not every Christian feels called to participate in peace demonstrations or to commit civil disobedience. Personally I have always felt a strong hesitation to break any law. So far I have not yet felt called to be arrested and go to jail for the sake of peace. I have always wondered if going to jail would not alienate people from the cause of peace rather than attract them to it. But maybe I am too much concerned about influencing others and not enough about faithfulness to my own spiritual commitment. Frankly, I am not so sure whether it is prudence or cowardice, conviction or practicality, faithfulness or fear that holds me back. I only know that what seemed so alien and unacceptable to me a few years ago now presents itself as at least an invitation to rethink my previous attitudes.

What should be clear in all this is that our differences of opinion about demonstrations and nonviolent civil disobedience should not be an argument for not working for peace. It is not important that all Christians act in the same way for peace or even agree on every style of peacemaking. It is important that their varied actions are all done and experienced as a form of personal or communal prayer. Because only then can we be lifelong resisters. This resistance may mean participation in peace education programs. It may involve public speaking or writing. It may be a gentle response to a militaristic friend. It may even include visiting the sick, helping the hungry, or protecting the weak. But as long as such actions come forth from an angry, hostile heart they may do more harm than good. On the other hand, when they express gratitude for belonging to the house of God, we will no longer have to worry about whether they are fruitful, since what comes from God never returns to God empty.

It is hard to see how prayer can be fruitful unless it brings us into a new and creative relationship with people. It is also hard for me to see how resistance can be fruitful unless it deepens and strengthens our relationship with God. Prayer and resistance, the twin pillars of Christian peacemaking, are two interlocking ways of giving expression to the peace we have found in the dwelling place of God. They come from the same source and lead to the same goal.

The Nonviolent Way

Christian resistance is nonviolent, because the peace we want to bring is not of this world. It is brought not by enslaving our enemies, but by converting them; not by showing strength, but by sharing in the confession of a common weakness; not by becoming unapproachable, but by making oneself vulnerable; not by retaliation, but by turning the other cheek; not by violence, but by love.

Jesus shows the way. When Pilate asks him, "Are you the
king of the Jews?" Jesus responds: "Mine is not a kingdom of this world; if my kingdom were of this world, my
disciples would have fought to prevent my being surren-
dered to the Jews. But my kingdom is not of this kind"
(John 18:33–66). And he who could have asked and received more than twelve legions of angels to come to his
defense (see Matt. 26:53) chose to die on a cross, lonely,
naked, vulnerable, and defenseless. Jesus' way is the way
without curses, weapons, violence, or power. For him
there are no countries to be conquered, no ideologies to
be imposed, no people to be dominated. There are only
children, women, and men to be loved. And love does not
use weapons. Love is not made manifest in power but in
powerlessness.

Jesus challenges all his followers to take this way.
It is the way of disarmed, nonviolent, powerless resistance. Those who have chosen that way have discovered
its spiritual force. Cesar Chavez has said: "Once people
understand the strength of nonviolence — the force it gen-
erates, the love it creates, the response it brings from
the total community — they will not easily abandon it."
Martin Luther King Jr. explores this when he writes, "Returning violence for violence multiplies violence, adding
deeper darkness to a night already devoid of stars. Darkness cannot drive out darkness; only light can do that.
Hate cannot drive out hate; only love can do that."
This disarmed resistance through love becomes possible
when we no longer look at the world through the eyes
of fear, suspicion, and insecurity, but through the eyes

of God, who loves every human being with infinite and unconditional love.

The resistance that brings peace does not divide the world into friends to be protected and enemies to be crushed. God has invited us to his dwelling place where such distinctions are unknown. There indeed is only one way of peacemaking and that is God's way. And God's way is the disarmed way, made known to us through the death of Jesus. By following this way — the way of love, the way of peace, the way of the cross — we become God's children. "Blessed are the peacemakers," Jesus proclaims, "for they will be called children of God" (Matt. 5:9).

To resist hatred, division, conflict, war, and death is indeed divine worship. Writing about nonviolence, André Trocmé, the great French Christian pacifist, says: "Nonviolence is above all a witness to God. Should nonviolence become a mere method to 'gain the whole world,' it would quickly be used by political parties to ends of dubious integrity. And then what would be left of it?"

Not without Opposition

Nonviolent resistance, however, is not a way that will find an easy acceptance. On the contrary, those who see violence as the only and necessary way to peace will not only consider nonviolent resisters unrealistic and naïve, but also treat them as cowards, conspirators with the enemy, and betrayers of the national cause. Nonviolent resisters are a great threat to those who wield power, since they suggest that there is another reality than the one they manipulate and try to force on others. And just as Jesus in his total disarmament evoked the ridicule and rage of the authorities of his time, so too will anyone who thinks, speaks, or acts according to the conviction that peace is not made by the sword.

Jesus leaves little doubt that the resister will not be unwelcome in this world. "Men will seize you and persecute you; they will hand you over to the synagogues and to imprisonment, and bring you before kings and governors because of my name" (Luke 21:12). "If the world hates you, remember that it hated me before you.... If they persecuted me, they will persecute you too" (John 15:18, 20).

Those who have come to know and belong to God have made themselves strangers to this world. Their "No" and their "Yes" will not be understood by those who are fighting. On the contrary, they will evoke anger, hostility, and aggression, for the message of peace is not welcome in our world. I have little doubt that as nonviolent peacemakers continue to do what they are now doing, they will be persecuted, maltreated, and thrown into jail in increasing numbers.

The closer we come to war, the harsher will peacemakers be treated. The greater the need for popular support of war efforts, the more ruthlessly resisters will be treated. Once I heard an American Christian say to a Korean minister: "You went to prison and suffered long for your conviction, but what can we who live such comfortable lives here in the U.S. do for peace?" The Korean smiled gently and said: "If you just continue to act as a Christian, you will soon be where I was!" So far the courts in this country have been very lenient and at times even tolerant toward war resisters. But when the powers preparing for war make peacemakers look more and more like enemies of the people, the day may come when antinuclear demonstrators will face consequences quite different than arrest by polite police officers and an overnight stay in jail.

Not Alone but Together

If life is going to be harder for those who say "No" to war and "Yes" to life, how then can Christian resisters and nonviolent peacemakers stay alive in this world? The simple answer is: together. As long as we look at resistance as performing individual acts of heroism, there won't be many peacemakers who will survive the enormous pressures put upon them. Resistance that makes for peace is not so much the effort of brave and courageous individuals as the work of the community of faith. Individual people, even the best and the strongest, will soon be exhausted and discouraged. But a community of resistance can persevere even when its members have their moments of weakness and despair. Peacemaking can be a lasting work only when we live and work together. Community is indispensable for a faithful and enduring resistance. Without community we will be quickly sucked back into the dark world of needs and wounds, of violence and destruction, of evil and death. For that reason, I now need to speak about community as the third characteristic of a spirituality of peacemaking.

III

COMMUNITY

Prayer and resistance can be expressions of Christian peacemaking only when they are embedded in community. Without the context of community, prayer and resistance easily degenerate into forms of individual heroism. Thus, they share in the arrogance of those who believe peace can be achieved by fighting. When St. Paul speaks to Timothy about the last days he warns him: "People will be self-centered ... arrogant and rude ... they will keep up the outward appearance of religion but will have rejected the inner power of it" (2 Tim. 3:1–5). We may be quite "prayerful" and involved in all sorts of resistance, but in a society with so many "enemies of everything that is good" (2 Tim. 3:3) even our most religious behavior can become an expression of arrogance, allowing us to satisfy our inner cravings under the illusion that we are pleasing God. We too can easily become "treacherous and reckless, and demented with pride, preferring [our] own pleasure to God" (2 Tim. 3:4). Precisely when we are threatened by nuclear extinction the danger of being deceived by sensation seekers is so great that peacemaking can easily turn into its opposite.

For that reason, it is important that the house of God's peace, the divine dwelling place, be made visible in a new human community. Only when we belong to a supportive, as well as self-critical, community is there a chance that our peacemaking effort may be more God-serving than self-serving.

Community, however, offers more than simply a protective context for prayer and resistance. It is also the first realization of the "new heavens and the new earth" (2 Pet. 3:13). It is not just a means to accomplish peace; it is the place where the peace we are seeking receives its first form.

Confession and Forgiveness

When you walk through the streets and avenues of any American city, travel by subway or bus, or wait in a train station or airport, it strikes you how isolated we human beings have become. No words of greeting meet you, no gestures of mutual recognition — not even a smile. People move quickly to some unknown destination. They hide themselves behind a book or newspaper, they eat standing alone behind a little one-person table, they do not speak. It seems as if they live in an invisible cage that protects them from their surroundings. Their bodies are tense, their eyes fearful, their whole way of being reflects a suspicious attitude.

Constantly reminded of the dangers around us, we may gradually lose trust in our fellow human beings and live as if we were in enemy territory, surrounded by people interested only in our destruction. What is happening to our world? It seems that the "sovereignties and powers, who originate the darkness in this world, the spiritual army of evil" (Eph. 6:12) have invaded our society in such a pervasive way that all of us, against our wills, have become their victims. We do not want to be afraid of people on the street, but we are. We do not want to lock our car, bike, or house over and again, but we do. We do not like to warn our parents, children, and friends not to go out on the streets alone, but we do. We do not believe that everyone around us is our enemy, but we behave as if they are. And suddenly we realize that we have become strangers in our own land: fearful, isolated, and powerless. Instead of self-confidence and freedom, we experience anxiety and paralysis. Instead of hope and joy, we feel an inner emptiness and sadness.

The enemy — the one we hold at bay with our intercontinental ballistic missiles, our B-52 bombers, and our Trident submarines — has already conquered our hearts and minds and has already been able to divide us among ourselves. We start to sense that the nuclear arms race is somehow a sign of the tragic disintegration of our own society. The higher we build our walls the more we hide the misery behind them. Our common enemy helps us to avoid facing the fact that there is no longer peace among ourselves.

The greatest tragedy of our time is our isolation. Young children feel lonely and unable to find friends, adolescents band together to have some sense of belonging, young families don't know their neighbors. Men and women work in offices under neon lights, sitting behind metal desks, drinking instant coffee from paper cups, eating their lunch out of a paper bag, and often wondering if they make any contribution at all. Retired people feel useless and rejected. The elderly are discarded in nursing homes with an occasional visit as their only consolation, while the many who die alone have become silent witnesses to the all-pervasive isolation that keeps our world in its claws. How can we still deny the power of evil? How can we laugh at those who warn that the devil is "prowling around like a roaring lion, looking for someone to devour" (1 Pet. 5:8–9)?

It is into this world that Jesus Christ brings his peace. This is the world in which we are challenged to make that divine peace manifest. If we try to do it alone, on our own initiative and with our own resources, we only perpetrate the isolation in which we are caught. Jesus himself did not suggest that we should go into this world as heroes, fighting the demons alone. No, he sent us his divine Spirit, who brings us together in one body, a body of very different people, united by the same promise and set free for the same work of peace. That new body is Christ's own body, present at all times and at all places. This is the great mystery of the Christian community. It is the living Christ, bringing his peace to those who want to be free from their isolation, mutual suspicion, and fear. And it is this living body of the Christian community that is able to oppose the powers and principalities that roam around this world. When peacemakers are not part of community, they are not part of the living Christ, and their peace is a false peace.

But if the Christian community is so essential for peace-making, what then makes us part of such a community? First, we have to discard all our tendencies to identify community with places, organizations, and denominations. As long as we associate community with a house, a convent, a parish church, a club, a congregation, a social agency, or a voluntary organization, we move away from its true spiritual meaning. Community life may take place in buildings and organizations, but these buildings and organizations are not the substance of community. I would say that even friendships, marriages, families, and households do not necessarily form Christian community. They all can be part of it, but they do not constitute the center. What makes a Christian community is a life of mutual confession and mutual forgiveness in the name of Jesus. Christian community is a faithful fellowship of the weak in which, through a repeated confession and forgiveness of sins, the strength of Jesus Christ is revealed and celebrated. Christian community is the spiritual place where people come together to recognize that Jesus Christ is Lord, a recognition which becomes possible only by a willingness to live in shared vulnerability. A Christian community is a gathering of people who manifest the peace of Christ by disclaiming their ability to make peace on their own. A Christian community is a place where strength is revealed in weakness, faith is revealed in the recognition of doubt, hope is revealed by the honest realization of moments of despair, love is revealed amid the reality of jealousy, suspicion, and distrust, joy is revealed in the midst of sadness, and peace is revealed within the humble awareness of violence, conflicts, and divisions. Indeed, Christian community is nothing less than Jesus Christ revealed among us sinful men and women.

Confession and forgiveness stand in the center of the mission of Jesus. John the Baptist points to Jesus as the "lamb of God that takes away the sins of the world" (John 1:29), and the whole of Jesus' ministry is a proclamation of God's forgiveness. Forgiveness is the great divine gift offered to us by Jesus. It is not a human possibility to forgive sins. "Who can forgive sins but God alone?" (Luke 5:21), Jesus' critics rightly ask. Wherever Jesus goes he offers this divine forgiveness. He even offers it to those who kill him. It is for the forgiveness of sins that he pours out his blood on the cross (Matt. 26:28) and that he sends forth his disciples into the world. The mission of peace is a mission of forgiveness of sins. It is the mission by which fear is overcome and a new order is inaugurated. This becomes very clear in one of Jesus' last appearances. When the disciples were fearfully gathered together behind closed doors, "Jesus came and stood among them. He said to them 'Peace be with you. As the Father sent me so am I sending you.' After saying this he breathed on them and said: 'Receive the Holy Spirit. For those whose sins you forgive they are forgiven; for those whose sins you retain, they are retained'" (John 20:19–23).

This forgiveness of sins becomes the mark of the Christian community. The willingness to forgive each other is the sign of God's forgiveness. This is what Jesus himself made clear: "If you forgive others their failings, your heavenly Father will forgive you yours" (Matt. 6:14). Such forgiveness is not simply a one-time event. No, it is a never-ending forgiveness, a forgiveness that character- izes the daily life of the Christian. When Peter asks Jesus, "Lord how often must I forgive my brother if he wrongs me? As often as seven times?" Jesus answers: "Not seven, I tell you, but seventy-seven times" (Matt. 18:21–22).

What then is required to obtain forgiveness? The answer is *repentance*. Repentance means the humble con- fession of our sinfulness. All through the New Testament we hear the word "Repent." The first words we hear Jesus say are "Repent and believe in the Good News" (Mark 1:15), and his last words recorded by Luke are: "It is written that the Christ would suffer and on the third day rise from the dead, and that, in his name, repentance for the forgiveness of sins would be preached to all nations" (Luke 24:47). Confession of sins is the concrete form of repentance. Jesus requires first and foremost that we recognize our need for forgiveness. With irony he says: "I did not come to call the virtuous, but the sinners." Only those who are willing to see themselves as sinners can be open to receiving the divine gift of forgiveness. Thus it is clear that mutual confession and forgiveness are the mark of our life together as Christians. That is because it is precisely in this continuous process of con- fession and forgiveness that we are liberated from our isolation and encounter the possibility of a new disarmed way of living. Christians are peacemakers not when they apply some special skill to reconcile people with one an- other but when, by the confession of their brokenness, they form a community through which God's unlimited forgiveness is revealed to the world. Community emerges when we dare to overcome our fears and confess to each other how much we still belong to the world. When that happens the light of God's forgiveness can shine brightly, and true peace can appear. Sometimes this takes place among friends, or between spouses. Sometimes we see it in religious houses. Sometimes it happens between denominations and churches, or even between peoples and countries. Then dividing lines dissolve, long-standing differences — whether religious or ethnic — no longer stand in the way of lasting fellowship. Every time this happens community takes root.

There is no better way to test our commitment to peacemaking than by locating our real community. Maybe we will find that we are not living a life of community at all. Then we have reason to wonder about the quality of our prayer and resistance. But wherever we find community we will find a disarmed, nonviolent way of being together, a way of life in which the sting of death (1 Cor. 15:55) is constantly removed and the new forces of life made visible.

Confession and forgiveness are the spiritual pillars on which the Christian community rests. They are the God-given way to break through the many boundaries of fear that keep us separated from each other and that isolate us in our self-protective cocoons. Every time we have the courage to say, "I have sinned against God and against you by loving the darkness more than the light, and I ask for forgiveness," we make a choice for reconciliation instead of self defense and we set our feet on the way of peace (Luke 1:7–9). It is not an easy way, since our fears and sadness keep whispering: "Don't make a fool of yourself, don't give the others a chance to get ahead of you, don't be naïve and show your weakness. . . . " But this is not the voice of him who "emptied himself to assume the condition of a slave" (Phil. 2:7). It is the voice that comes out of our darkness and wants to seduce us to build more walls, to buy more weapons, and to prevent a war by starting one.

Nevertheless, every time we choose the way of confession and forgiveness we catch a glimpse of the place that the Lord has prepared for us (John 14:2). It might be a matter of small choices: a letter written to restore a broken relationship, a gentle word to an angry friend, an offer to take the last place, a note of praise to a competitor, an invitation to talk, a willingness to make the first move, to offer a handshake, an embrace, or a kiss. These and many other choices call forth the community of love, not just between individuals, but between peoples and nations as well. They are more than signs of good will. They are the first realization of the new heaven and the new earth we are awaiting.

Seeds of Hope

Belonging to a community of confession and forgiveness radically changes our lives as resisters. Not only does it take away our sense of isolation, but it also offers us new courage and new confidence. When we read the daily papers with their grim stories about the world situation, we may come to wonder why our world still exists. Every day new and more destructive arms are developed, and each day offers new excuses for their use. The news about the Middle East, Afghanistan, Central America, Iran, and many African countries, the horrifying stories about contemporary slavery, execution, mass murder, torture, and other forms of exploitation make us wonder if there is any way to avoid the coming holocaust that will put an end to our human history. So inundated are we with bad news — day in day out, year after year — that we easily surrender to a mood of resignation. What we hear, see, and read is so discouraging that we are constantly tempted to throw up our arms and say: "The world is simply rushing to the edge of a cliff. Who can stop it? If we don't see the end of the world, our children will. Why do anything at all?"

But defeatism and despair are contrary to everything for which Jesus Christ came, particularly the gift of hope. He did not offer optimism based on statistics, political analysis, the balance of power, deterrence, or first-strike capability, but hope based on the promise of God's forgiveness to all people. This hope becomes visible in the community of those who believe in God's power to forgive. This is something quite different from a general expectation that things will eventually work out. It is the concrete living out of faith in the living God, a faith stronger than violence, oppression, hunger, war, or the assumption of "mutually assured destruction." It is people coming together to work for the new kingdom and to announce the light "that darkness could not overpower" (John 1:4). This community is able to resist the powers of death and evil because it is the living Christ himself present in the world. The Christian community is the living representation of the risen Lord. It is a sign of hope precisely since it represents the light that cannot be extinguished and the life that cannot be killed. To belong to the Christian community is to be free from the powers that rule the world. This is truly the source of all resistance. The Christian community is not a group of people who have come together to unify their forces and thus make victory more likely. No, it is the expression of a victory already won. St. Paul says, "Death is swallowed up in victory" (1 Cor. 15:54), and John tells his disciples, "Anyone who has been begotten by God, has already overcome the world" (1 John 5:4). Thus the hope of those who belong to the living Christ is a hope rooted in what has already occurred, even if the total fullness of this event has not yet been revealed. Thus the Christian community, wherever it emerges, marks a new world in the midst of the old, of light in the midst of darkness, of life in the midst of death.

It is precisely this victorious quality of the Christian community that makes it a true community of resistance. Only as members of that community can our resistance have real spiritual significance.

What does a community of resistance look like today? Do we have any models? All through history we see how new Christian communities emerged in response to the problems of their time. In the sixth century the new community of St. Benedict responded to the fall of the Roman Empire and offered a new way of thinking and living that would give shape and form to the Europe of the Middle

Ages. In the thirteenth century we see the Franciscan communities develop and set a new tone in response to the wealth and decadence of the medieval church. And how could we ever understand the issues and problems of our day without the profound influence of the many Christian communities inspired by the reformers of the sixteenth century? Confession and forgiveness may have had different contents during these different periods of history, yet they always led to a new affirmation of the risen Lord, the Lord of history, who conquered the forces of death.

How will we respond today? Never before have we been confronted with a power that can end history itself. Never before have we been asked to respond as Christians to a threat of collective suicide. Never before have we been challenged to affirm the risen Lord when the world he overcame has seemed so bent on self-destruction. In the face of the human ability to extinguish all that is human, what does it mean to think about faith, hope, love, and life everlasting? God has been revealed as a loving father, guiding his children through history. But what if history no longer can be counted on as the framework of our understanding of God's love? Jesus is the son of God who became flesh for our sake and dwelled among us. But what if we are contemplating ways to burn all human flesh in a worldwide holocaust? The Spirit is the spirit of the living God who transforms the old earth into a new earth and makes everything new. But what if there is nothing left to be transformed and made new? Can we really think about Father, Son, and Holy Spirit if all relationships that give shape to the human family are threatened? Can we really speak about birth, death, and resurrection when fecundity itself is in question? Can we talk about heaven and hell when we can no longer be sure that the earth is going to exist much longer? Can we direct our eyes in faith and hope toward God when we are shaken in our basic trust in the humanity of people?

We face a threat qualitatively different from all other previous threats and we do not have a fitting model for a response. A new order, a new rule, a new reformation, a new spiritual leader — none of these "solutions" seems to have the power to give us the hope we seek. As humanity we have entered a period in which our faith is being stripped of all support systems and defense mechanisms. But it is precisely with this naked faith that we are called to build a community of hope that is able to resist the darkness of our age.

When I think of this new community in our time I think about people from all over the world reaching out to each other in total vulnerability. In my mind's eye I see a worldwide network of men and women so totally disarmed that they not only have given up the power of weapons but also religious concepts, symbols, and institutions. I see them moving over this world, visiting each other, binding each other's wounds, confessing their brokenness to each other, and forgiving each other with a simple word, an embrace, a touch, or even a smile. I see them walking alone or together in the most simple clothes caring for the sick, feeding the hungry, comforting the lonely, and waiting quietly with the dying. I see them in apartment buildings, farm houses, schools and universities, hospitals, and office buildings as quiet witnesses of God's presence. Wherever they are they bring peace, not as much by what they say or do, but mostly by their connectedness with those others with whom they form a new community of hope.

All these people are in the world but no longer belong to it. They need each other to remain faithful to their vocation as peacemakers. They need each other to make their lives an unceasing prayer to God. They need each other for inspiration, for material and moral support. They need each other to remain joyful and grateful. But most of all they need each other to form together the living body of Christ in the midst of this nuclear world. Every time they come together they pray. Whenever possible they visit each other and write each other. In times of crisis they consult each other and ask each other's advice to find the right response. Sometimes they act together, but not always. Occasionally they become visible and outspoken, but more often they live like contemplatives. They are held together by a rule, a rule of faith, hope, and love rooted in the Gospel of Jesus. They are accountable to each other, always open for criticism and new directions. Their main concern is to do the will of God and not their own. Thus they spend much time and energy carefully discerning what type of life or action they are called to. They are clusters of peacemakers in different parts of the world, but there are also individual members of the community of resistance who live alone or far from the center of action. The presence of the community is hardly known to the news media. Once in a while they attract attention because of a publication, a demonstration, or an act of civil disobedience, but usually they merge with the larger society. They are quiet, prayerful, and gentle people. They are not panicky, restless, angry, or hostile. At least they try not to be. As often as possible they come together for days of study, reflection, and prayer. Sometimes these days are used to prepare for a concrete peace witness, but mostly they are to strengthen the bond of love and peace with their Lord and with each other.

Outsiders think of them as members of a new order, but they are different from the old orders. They are men and women, celibates and married people, young and old; they come from different churches and denominations, and they live in very different places. However, they all are peacemakers, sons and daughters of God united in their deep commitment to bring the peace of Christ to this world. Together they say "No" to evil and death and together they affirm life whenever and wherever they can. In this worldwide community of resistance emerging in the face of a nuclear threat the old message becomes new again. Words that had lost their meaning receive new strength, old symbols reveal their power to communicate, ideas that were no longer taken seriously are gradually used again to say what needs to be said. Meanwhile, new words, new symbols, and new ideas are developing and being tested. There is an exhilarating sense that a new house is being built, a house of peace, a dwelling place for God, a temple of the most high. The stones are the people of God, stones shining brightly in the sun. And as this temple is being noticed far and wide, more and more people leave their warmaking world behind and go up to the new temple. On their way they take off their helmets and let their weapons fall by the side of the road. Their tense eyes relax and start looking around, their hands no longer grasp but gently touch the hands of others, and gradually as they go up to the house of the Lord their shouting becomes singing, and their voices unite with other voices. Then the world hears what it has not heard for a long time.

> *How lovely is your dwelling place*
> *Lord, God of hosts.*
> *My soul is longing and yearning,*
> *is yearning for the courts of the Lord.*
> *My heart and my soul ring out their joy*
> *to God, the living God. . . .*
>
> *They are happy, who dwell in your house,*
> *forever singing your praise.*
> *They are happy, whose strength is in you,*
> *in whose hearts are the roads to Zion.*
>
> (Psalm 84, Grail translation)

Thus, a new earth is being fashioned and the community of resistance becomes a community of praise and thanksgiving.

Gratitude

The community of peacemakers is not only the place of resistance but also the place of prayer. But neither prayer nor resistance can be understood in their full significance outside the context of community life. Both are expressions of a confidence in the risen Lord. The resurrection of Jesus as celebrated in the life of the Christian community is much more than a past event joyfully commemorated in the present. It is an event that is recognized as a continuing reality within the life of the community itself. Therefore resistance can never be an anxious attempt to prevent something terrible from happening. On the contrary, it is a "No" that flows forth from the true presence of the Lord, who says: "I am the Life" (John 14:6). Therefore, too, prayer can never be a panicky request to avoid disaster. In the daily life of the community prayer is first of all an expression of thanks for what we already have received.

A life in community is a life lived in unceasing gratitude to the Lord with whom we dwell. Community reveals that true prayer always moves us to thanksgiving for what already has been given us. Even a cry for God's help cannot be separated from a spirit of gratitude. Jesus himself explains this when he says: "In your prayers do not babble as the pagans do, for they think that by using many words they will makes themselves heard. Do not be like them; your Father knows what you need before you ask him" (Matt. 6:7–8). We do not ask to convince a hesitant giver. We do not beg for help from someone who needs to be convinced of our need. We ask the giver of all good who loves us so much that he won't hold anything from us that we need. As a community of faith we remind each other constantly that we need to be grateful even when we suffer, even when we feel downcast, even when things only seem to be getting worse. We can do this because we know that the world in which we suffer has already been overcome. This victory allows us to be grateful at all times and at all places. Before his death Jesus told his disciples about the rejection and persecution that would mark their lives, but he also told them that their suffering would not rob them of their peace. "In the world, you will have trouble," he said, "but be brave. I have conquered the world" (John 16:33).

If there is any word that should characterize the life of peacemakers, it is "gratitude." True peacemakers are grateful persons, persons who constantly recognize and celebrate the peace of God within and among them. This might at first sound sentimental, but those who have lived through periods of true pain and agony know the mystery of gratitude. They have come to experience that where they meet the suffering Christ they also meet the Christ of peace. Whenever our suffering becomes his suffering and our agony his agony we know in our innermost being that suffering and agony will not be able to destroy our gratitude since we have found our peace in him, a peace that is not of this world. To say thanks in the face of a nuclear holocaust threatening our planet with the extinction of all human life may seem ridiculous. But when we realize that Christ also suffered this nuclear agony and anguish and overcame it on the cross, then our gratitude can be even deeper and stronger.

When we try to face the demons of violence and destruction alone, we quickly feel powerless. This experience of powerlessness easily leads to an inner rage and when this becomes a lasting emotion it settles within us as resentment. Resentment is the opposite of gratitude. It is the mood of a hardened heart that no longer waits for anything new and has accepted death as a fatality that cannot be escaped. Resentment is thus a sign of our having become victims of the darkness of this world and of having lost faith in the One who is the light. Gratitude, however, becomes possible when we no longer have to deal with the world on our own but have found the living Christ in our life together and can show each other in every concrete way that something new is happening. Those who live in a community of confession and forgiveness always say thanks. Their life together, whether this involves physical closeness or not, is a life in which they help others see where the risen Lord of peace appears and shows his glorified wounds. It is remarkable to notice how gratitude can burst forth wherever true peacemakers work together in community. They open each other's eyes to the treasures in their midst, treasures that they never would have discovered on their own.

I remember how I once went to Peru in order to respond to the enormous needs of the people. The stories about their poverty and hunger, their lack of medical care and education, had made me so restless that I felt a deep urge to offer my help in whatever way I could. People who heard of my plans considered me courageous and generous. But when I lived for some time among the people something very different took place. The ministers, priests, and sisters I lived with opened my eyes to the countless gifts the Peruvian poor had to offer me. They made me see how much joy there was amid all the sadness and how much care there was amid all the oppression. They took me to the most poverty-stricken neighborhoods and let me enter the most miserable-looking hovels. But what they wanted me to see was not just poverty, misery, and oppression, but people who had something to give, something beautiful. They opened my eyes to the most human qualities of humanity: friendship, parenthood, mutual support, playfulness, trust, the ability to respond faithfully to tragedy, and endless other gifts that had remained hidden from me. When I finally said that I would like to work with these people, I realized that my motivation should be not their poverty but their gifts, not their great needs but their great talents. I came to see that helping the poor should be first and foremost an act of gratitude. As long as I worked there because of my guilty conscience or my sense that they needed me, I would not be a real peacemaker, but when I could be with them to exchange gifts and live gratefully it could become a relationship without limits.

Working to prevent a nuclear war should not be different. As long as our restlessness, anxiety, and feelings of guilt dominate our work as peacemakers we cannot last long. But when we have opened each other's eyes to the great human gifts among all people we can indeed make peacemaking a way of being. The greatest service we can offer each other is mutual support in our conversion from resentment to gratitude. The politicians, the military, and the civilians who are part of the gigantic nuclear enterprise are not evil people. They are men and women who do their best to live an honest life, and frequently experience their work as a real service. Often they are fearful and worried people, who feel that an increase in defense spending is the only realistic way to save us all from total destruction by the power of the enemy.

As a community of peacemakers it is our task first of all to recognize and affirm the great human gifts these people too carry within themselves. We have to see them as caring, loving, concerned human beings who, like us, desire peace and freedom, even if preparation for war is their way to achieve it. Just as we have to confess our own dark forces to each other, so do we have to reveal the gifts of peace in those whose lives and works we hope to change. When these people too recognize that they have real talents for peacemaking within and among them, they may become free enough to let go of their fears and claim their ability to live together as brothers and sisters without guns, bombs, B-52s, cruise missiles, and Trident submarines.

Thus the community of peacemaking is a Eucharistic community. The word "eucharist" means gratitude. Wherever peacemakers speak and act, their words and actions announce the "good grace" (*eu* = good, *charis* = grace) of God. Therefore the eucharist belongs to the center of the communal life of peacemakers. It is the event in which all peacemaking is summarized. A little piece of bread and a small cup of wine are taken and shared and Jesus' words are spoken: "This is my body, this is my blood." Thus we take from the earth what sustains us and lift it up to him who makes it his own. Small, insignificant human gifts become God's greatest gift, the gift of himself to all of us. We give God part of ourselves; he gives us all of himself. We ask God to understand our hunger and thirst; he gives us more than we even asked for. We express a reasonable desire; he responds to a desire greater than we were aware of, a desire to dwell forever in his house and share in his table. We make a small gesture of gratitude, and he shows us the limitless of his generosity. Then we see that all is a pure unconditional gift. Then we realize that air and sea, forests and canyons, rivers and mountains, fields and deserts, birds and all animals, babies, children, teenagers, men and women of all ages, races, and religions — all are manifestations of that inexhaustible divine generosity. Every time we break bread and share the cup with people from all over this fearful war-torn world we say to each other: "All is given, brother; all is given, sister; all is given . . . just lift up your heads to him who gives and be grateful." Then people know that they do not have to hoard anything any longer, that they do not have to defend anything any longer, that they do not have to fight over anything any longer. All is given freely by a lover so generous that no human being lacks for anything. Is there any condition, any prerequisite? Not really. We just have to recognize life for what it is: a gift to be grateful for, not a property to cling to, hoard, or defend. All that is asked of us is to believe that we are loved so fully, so deeply, and so unreservedly that God's abundance is ours.

This is what the community of peacemakers is about. It proclaims God's endless generosity; it reminds us that all we have to do is say thanks for all that we have received. When words of thanks come from every corner of the world, then boundaries between peoples will vanish and then we all will lift up our eyes to him from whom all good things come. Then we will see that he loves us all in the most intimate way and has created us to be brothers and sisters within that richly varied human family. Then indeed we can sit together around the same table and say: "How good and how pleasant it is / When brothers [and sisters] live in unity" (Ps. 133:1).

When these sounds of gratitude are heard, the sounds of war will fall silent. People will look at each other and tears will come to their eyes when they realize that once they spent all their time and energy to build a hell in which they could burn each other. Then the missiles will rust away in their silos, the submarines will decay, and the bombers will be put in museums to remind children that once there were savage times.

This is indeed the vision of peacemakers. As peacemakers we are not blind to the reality that surrounds us. We do not deny the nuclear threat and the possibility that human beings will put an end to their own history. We will even alert friends and strangers to the most dangerous predicament our planet has ever known. But what makes us peacemakers is not threats or fears but the vision of the new and holy city coming down from heaven, the city of peace, the city without pain and agony, the city in which God will make his home among us. This vision is not a faraway utopian dream. It is a vision that is already being realized among us here and now in our

Eucharistic community. It is a vision of the Lord-with-us in the midst of the sounds and spectacles of war. "Happy are the eyes that see what you see," Jesus says, "for I tell you that many kings and prophets wanted to see what you see, and never saw it" (Luke 10:23–24). Thus our hope is based on what we already see, and what we see gives us always new courage to work for the day of the Lord when all powers of evil will be put under his feet and he will reign forever. With this glorious vision, how can we be but grateful?

To reiterate, community is essential for peacemaking. By confessing our own anger, lust, hostility, and violence to each other and by offering again and again God's forgiveness to each other, a community of peace can emerge among us. This community, whose members boast of their weakness but trust in God's strength, can offer true resistance against the forces of darkness. This community too can lift up to God the gifts of life in an unceasing prayer of thanksgiving. The community of peacemakers, therefore, is much more than a supportive context for peace activists. It is that joyful and grateful place where the new Jerusalem becomes visible. It is the Jerusalem toward which we travel always, but it is also the Jerusalem whose peace we already know in our heart. From this community the song goes up:

> *I rejoiced when I heard them say:*
> *"Let us go to God's house."*
> *And now our feet are standing*
> *Within your gates, O Jerusalem....*

For the peace of Jerusalem pray:
"Peace be to your homes!
May peace reign in your walls,
In your palaces peace!"

For love of my brethren and friends
I say: "Peace upon you!"
For love of the house of the Lord
I will ask for your good.

(Psalm 122)

CONCLUSION

"Blessed are the peacemakers, for they will be called children of God" (Matt. 5:9). These words of Jesus are the basis of this book. They are words with universal and timeless validity, but in a society that is busy constructing every day more nuclear warheads and in an age that offers countless opportunities to use them, they have become the key words for our lives as Christians today.

In this book I have tried to develop a spirituality for peacemakers. I have tried to look at our vocation to live in the Spirit of Jesus Christ from the perspective of our growing awareness that peace is the issue. Ever since the twelve apostles preached the Good News of Jesus to all people, prayer, resistance, and community have been considered indispensable elements of the Christian life. But when we look at them in a time threatened by the end of time, they receive a significance they couldn't have had before. In our nuclear predicament, prayer comes to mean ultimate survival, resistance comes to mean a radical "No" to a world engulfing death, and community comes to mean the beginning of a spiritual home that no cruise missile or Trident submarine can destroy. To live a life in the

Spirit of Christ today means to opt for a way of being in the world that in no way pays tribute to the forces of destruction. It means an uncompromising refusal to belong to the powers that try to push our planet into oblivion. It means a total belonging to the crucified and risen Lord.

The main thesis of this book has been that this total belonging to Christ is not an escape from the world, but the only way to be in the world as peacemakers. Only by belonging to Christ and to him alone, that is, only by living as brothers and sisters of Jesus and sons and daughters of God, can we truly resist the devastating powers of evil and work together in this world to avoid a collective suicide. If we ever will be able to prevent a nuclear holocaust and lead our human society on the road to disarmament, it will not be because we were so adept at denouncing deterrence or first-strike strategies, but because we have found our place in the house of God. Those who do not belong to this world are the only ones who can bring it the peace it craves. Those whose lives are securely anchored beyond the powers and principalities that rule the world can enter that world freely and bring it peace.

This does not mean that we should disdain political or socioeconomic strategies. To the contrary, they can be the concrete ways of being in the world. Lobbying, disarmament campaigns, antipoverty programs, and other peace activities are indispensable for a better world. There is no place for a mountaintop spirituality in the Gospel of Jesus. But in all these activities we have to be guided by the words of St. Paul: "Whatever you do at all, do it for

the glory of God" (1 Cor. 10:31). The first and final crite-
rion is whether we belong to God or to the world, whether
we live in the house of peace or in the dwelling places of
those who plot wars. There is little "piety" to this crite-
rion. It requires detachment from the world. It requires
a willingness to not let desire for success, popularity, or
power guide our behavior. It requires a single-minded
commitment to the Lord of peace even when that leads
to rejection, persecution, and even death. Since the survival of humanity itself is at stake, there is no half-way
solution. Jesus' words, "Who does not gather with me,
scatters," are more challenging than ever before.

In this book I have tried to give hope to peacemakers.
I have tried not to base my hope on the prediction that
we will be able to avoid a nuclear holocaust. There is
little reason for optimism these days. The powers involved
seem so bent on creating a conflict that any human being
with common sense knows that only a small mistake is
needed to set off an indescribable catastrophe. I have tried
to say, however, that we can look at the possibility of a
nuclear war and work with all we have to prevent it from
happening while at the same time trusting that we are
secure in the hands of the living God.

There our hope is anchored. I have used the image
of God's house to convey this sense of spiritual belonging that no human anger or greed can destroy. St. James
speaks about the same thing when he refers to the wisdom
from above in which we as peacemakers participate. He
says: "Wherever you find jealousy and ambition, you find
disharmony and wicked things of every kind being done;

whereas the wisdom that comes from above is something pure; it also makes for peace, and it is kindly and considerate; it is full of compassion and shows itself by doing good; nor is there any trace of partiality or hypocrisy in it. Peacemakers, when they work for peace, sow the seeds which will bear fruit in holiness" (James 3:16).

Holiness, that is, life with the Holy One, is the fruit of all peacemaking. Peacemakers come from God and they return to God with the fruits of their labor. Their home is God's home, their wisdom is God's wisdom, their love is God's love. They have found this home, this wisdom, and this love in and through their Lord Jesus Christ, who came from God to bring peace to this world, and who returned to God to bring all people with him as his sisters and brothers. The peace we have found is the peace that belongs to God. Christ is the first peacemaker since he opened the house of God to all people and thus made the old creation new. We are sent to this world to be peacemakers in his name. This is what St. Paul means when he speaks about reconciliation: "For anyone who is in Christ, there is a new creation: the old creation has gone, and now the new one is here. It is all God's work. It was God who reconciled us to himself through Christ and gave us the work of handing on this reconciliation. In other words, God in Christ was reconciling the world to himself, not holding men's faults against them, and he has entrusted to us the news that they are reconciled. So we are ambassadors for Christ; it is as though God were appealing through us, and the appeal that we make in Christ's name is: 'Be reconciled to God' " (2 Cor. 5:17–20).

"Be reconciled to God" — that means "Be at peace." This reconciliation and peace is God's gift to us in Jesus Christ, and no human being can destroy it. No country, no army, no president can deprive us of this divine peace. And this assurance allows us to be brave and resist with all our mental and spiritual energy the powers of death and to proclaim with great confidence that the Lord, Our God, is the Lord of peace.